D0929024

Ohio Outback

Ohio Outback

Learning to Love the Great Black Swamp

Claude Clayton Smith

The Kent State University Press

KENT, OHIO

© 2011 by The Kent State University Press, Kent, Ohio 44242
ALL RIGHTS RESERVED
Library of Congress Catalog Card Number 2010023511
ISBN 978-1-60635-054-6
Manufactured in the United States of America

LIBRARY OF CONGRESS CATALOGING-IN-PUBLICATION DATA
Smith, Claude Clayton, 1944–
Ohio outback : learning to love the great Black Swamp /
Claude Clayton Smith.
p. cm.
ISBN 978-1-60635-054-6 (hardcover : alk. paper) ∞
1. Smith, Claude Clayton, 1944——Homes and haunts.
2. Swamps—Maumee River Valley (Ind. and Ohio)
3. Authors, American—20th century—Biography. I. Title.
PS3569.M5165Z46 2011
813'.54—dc22
[B]
2010023511
British Library Cataloging-in-Publication data are available.

15 14 13 12 11   5 4 3 2 1

For my brothers—
Brian, Bob, and Bruce—
who chose to stay in Connecticut

outback—n. (out 'bak'). The hinterland of a given
country, usually Australia or New Zealand.
—*The American Heritage Dictionary*

Heaven is not one of your fertile Ohio bottoms,
you may depend on it.
—H. D. Thoreau

He wasn't a bad egg,
Just weak. He loved women and Ohio.
—John Ashbery

Contents

Acknowledgments

I am grateful to Joyce Harrison of the Kent State University Press for her enthusiastic interest in this collection from its earliest stages. I am grateful, too, to the editors of the following publications where several chapters appeared in slightly altered from: *Ohio Magazine* (1989, 1993); *The Gamut* (1989, 1990); *In Buckeye Country* (Bottom Dog Press, 1994); *Lapping America: A Man, a Corvette, and the Interstates* (Burford Books, 2006); *Wild Things* (Outrider Press, 2008); and *The Writer's Chronicle* (2009). The quotation by Jeffrey Hammond in the preface is from his article in the *American Scholar* (Summer 2001, p. 42). Descriptive words and phrases by Malcolm Cowley pertaining to *Winesburg, Ohio* in chapter 12 are from his introduction to that text (Viking, 1960, p. 15). The interstate item at the end of chapter 15 is from an Associated Press article by Mark Williams that appeared under the headline "I-670 Is End of the Road for Ohio" in the *Cincinnati Post* (July 2, 2003, p. A1).

As always, I am indebted to my wife, Elaine, who experienced the Ohio Outback with me, raising our children and reading these pages, one by one, as they were written.

Preface

When I moved my family to Ada, Ohio, in 1986, to take a teaching job at Ohio Northern University, our East Coast friends asked, "Where, exactly, do you live?" Well, I explained, Ohio's basically square (no pun intended), and we're in the center of the northwest quadrant, between the corn and the soybeans. To those who knew something about Ohio I added, "We're right in the middle of a triangle defined by Toledo, Columbus, and Dayton—that is to say, in the middle of nowhere." But that notion was qualified at our very first Town & Gown Banquet, hosted annually by the village of Ada and ONU, when one speaker averred, "Ada is in the middle of nowhere . . . and the center of everywhere." As native Ohioan Jeffrey Hammond points out, "In an attempt to sell more pralines, sausages, and gas, the state's tourism board . . . adopted the slogan: 'Ohio: The Heart of It All.' That's pretty catchy, but doesn't a heart pump blood elsewhere? And if you're the 'Heart,' then isn't the 'All' somewhere else?"

I am still wrestling with such questions after all these years.

I can't remember when I first began telling folks that we live in the Ohio Outback. It may have been after my wife and I saw two wonderful films set in rural Australia —*My Brilliant Career* and *The Man from Snowy River.* Or it may have been after the drought of 1988, when those two films could have been shot in the farmland and fields surrounding Ada. Adjusting to the local landscape was difficult enough without a drought, given that we had moved from the rolling green foothills of the Virginia Blue Ridge to the rectilinear flatness of Hardin County.

Nonetheless, the pieces in this book reflect a growing curiosity and fondness for Ohio. "Yard Wars of the Ohio Outback," a lighthearted memoir in twelve chapters, forms the book's narrative core. Before James Frey sullied the notion of the memoir with *A Million Little Pieces*, that form of creative nonfiction was "in," and so I thought I'd try my hand at it. And what better focus than one's own backyard, where the particular problems are at once indigenous and universal? "Yard Wars" details two decades of battling Nature in northwest Ohio. As such, it is my tribute to James Thurber, whose writing I included in my Great Works of Literature course during my twenty-year tenure at ONU, taking my students on field trips to the Thurber House in Columbus. What Thurber did for Columbus, I attempt to do for the Ohio Outback.

Interspersed throughout the "Yard Wars" narrative are six more journalistic pieces I wrote between 1988 and 2008. These begin right here in Ada, home of Wilson Sporting Goods Manufacturing Company and the NFL football. As luck would have it, one of my Ada neighbors, a supervisor at Wilson's, was able to arrange a tour of the plant for me shortly after we moved in, but it took me two more tours before I could write "Made in Ada: The NFL Ball," chronicling the complicated process of the birth of a professional football.

"Ditch Watch" grew out of my daily jogs to County Line Road, which divides Hardin County from Allen County to the west of us. In many ways this piece connects Ada to all of northwest Ohio, given the sophisticated system of ditches that ultimately carries our rain and runoff all the way to Lake Erie. But it is the people I met—as well as what I observed in the ditches—that informs "Ditch Watch," rooting my Hardin County neighbors in Ohio history.

"New Stark, Breathless" resulted from a question about New Stark on the old Route 30, the Lincoln Highway. Every time I passed through that place I was amused by its name, because New Stark, indeed, looked stark, making me wonder what *Old* Stark must have been like. I got to know the people there during the drought of 1988, nearly two decades before the new four-lane Route 30—parallel to the old—opened through fields just to the south. And so the piece is a record of life in New Stark when the traffic was still thick and fast.

In the fall of 1999, on sabbatical leave from ONU, I drove ten thousand miles around the perimeter of the forty-eight states solely on the interstates. My journey was a millennial tribute to the U.S. interstate system, the largest public works project in history. Beginning at home in Ada, I took I-75 north to Toledo, then circumnavigated the nation clockwise in a torch-red, 1996 Corvette, a vehicle symbolic— for better or worse—of the speed, power, wealth, style, and mobility of millennial America itself. En route I interviewed more than one hundred people as to their opinions of the interstate system, and in each corner of the country I planted a small millennial flag. My book *Lapping America* details that adventure, and "Ohio Interstate Take-off," adapted from its opening chapter, is included here.

"The Way to Winesburg" resulted from teaching Sherwood Anderson's *Winesburg, Ohio* (along with the writing of James Thurber) in my Great Works course and taking field trips with my students to Clyde, Anderson's hometown and the inspiration for his classic book. Although there is still a residue of resentment for Anderson abroad in Clyde due to his depiction of small-town Ohio life, I think that anyone who lives in such a town will discover—as my piece concludes— that "the way to Winesburg" is through your own backyard.

"Ohio Ringside: A Requiem for Boxing in the Buckeye State" stemmed from my experiences moonlighting as a licensed professional boxing judge in the state of Ohio. In 1988 I brought Joyce Carol Oates to ONU for a reading at a time when she was in the national limelight for her interviews with Mike Tyson, the undisputed and undefeated heavyweight champion of the world. Her book *On Boxing* had just been published. But Tyson's career soon soured, tarnishing Oates's reputation as well. In the years to follow, professional boxing in Ohio suffered a similar downward spiral, despite the more recent heroics of Vonda Ward, former heavyweight champion from Macedonia, or the undefeated (as of this writing) heavyweight Devin Vargas of Toledo, whose careers I have followed and whose fights I have judged.

Three pieces for this book were left unfinished. The first, to have been called "Saturday Night at the Red Dog Saloon," was abandoned after that roadside honky-tonk, on the outskirts of Roundhead on State Route 235, burned to the ground and was never rebuilt. It seemed the kind of place where hardworking guys come flying out the door to settle their differences in the parking lot. I cased the joint once when I stopped for lunch during the week, but the fire—rumored to have been arson—prevented me from witnessing the weekend action. The second piece involved a place called Jumbo, a small community of about a dozen trailer homes across from an abandoned grocery store at the intersection of State Routes 67 and 638. Local legend has it that the crossroads got its name when Jumbo the African elephant was buried there, having died as P. T. Barnum's circus passed through nearby Kenton on the train. I stopped in Jumbo once to investigate, but the local population, which is highly transient, hadn't heard of any dead elephant. Finally, I envisioned a piece called "The Buzzards of Hinckley, Ohio," about the annual return of turkey vultures to Hinckley Roost, just south of Cleveland, on the fifteenth of March. One dubious source attributes this phenomenon to a pile of Civil War corpses on which the ancestors of the present buzzards apparently feasted. But the annual "spotting"—only the sighting of the official spotter counts—seems rigged, so I never made the pilgrimage to experience this Ohio Outback version of the swallows of Capistrano.

In 2006 I took early retirement from ONU to work on my writing full time. If my wife and I were to stay in Ohio just one more year, I will have spent more of my life here than anywhere else, including my home state of Connecticut, where I grew up, attended college, and earned my first graduate degree. This precarious state (no pun intended) reminds me of a line I heard at a poetry reading not long after we moved to Ada—"Oh Lord, when I die," the poet joked, "please don't let me be from Ohio." Given the fact that I don't have as much time ahead of me on this planet as I've already put in (although I intend to live to the age of one hundred, just to be ornery), I am suddenly feeling the pressure to move—my wife and I would like to abandon our empty nest and be closer to our sons—lest we turn up our boots as Ohioans. Whether we move or not remains to be seen, but, as I point out in "Ditch Watch," a lovely country graveyard lies just around the corner from us on St. Paul Road, and the earth there is just as rich as any.

Yard Wars of the Ohio Outback

Christopher Horseshoe

Before we moved from southwest Virginia, Elaine did her homework. "All of Ohio was once forested," she said. "But pioneers clear-cut the area for farming with special techniques. They notched all the trees, so the fall of a single tree felled others like dominoes."

Then came the killer. "*Northwest* Ohio," she learned, "was known as the Great Black Swamp. It was Ohio's last frontier."

Oh no, I was thinking, because "swamp" means two things—mosquitoes and floods. Which we'd see our share of over the next twenty years. But first we had to unpack and settle in—to a housing development where trees cut by pioneers had been allowed to grow back—in the Ohio Outback between the corn and the soybeans.

The first home we owned in northwest Ohio was on Christopher Circle, a misnomer because it wasn't a circle. The street was laid out like a q, with a cul-de-sac at the left end of a straight stretch that came in from a road flanking the university where I'd be teaching in the fall. Our house, a relatively new ranch, faced the straight stretch of that q from the center of a narrow quarter-acre lot, the last on the left before the cul-de-sac. The cul-de-sac itself had a name—something suburban and pretty that I no longer remember—but our address, because the house faced west, was Christopher Circle.

Our street was called Christopher Circle because it was supposed to continue into the woods at the end of the straight stretch and circle back to the road flanking the university. But that plan had been foiled by a remnant of the Great Black Swamp that made it impossible to cut a road through those woods, let alone construct more houses. In any event, the original plan, from the perspective of the road flanking the university, would have created not a circle but an upside-down horseshoe. And, as anyone knows, an upside-down horseshoe brings bad luck.

Which is why we lived on Christopher Circle for just a year and a half.

The bad luck was twofold. First, our small, narrow lot was bordered by two streets—Christopher Circle to the west and the cul-de-sac to the south—neither of which had sidewalks or curbs. So our lawn went right up to the pavement. In this case, concrete.

Don't get me wrong—it was *the* place to live in our little university town, by far the loveliest development, with flowers and tall trees in everyone's backyard and real lawns, not crabgrass, out front. But the neighborhood was home to forty kids between the ages of three and eight, and there was absolutely no defense against them.

These kids flocked like pigeons, descending at a moment's notice, then moving on. They were already in the habit of cutting through our backyard—the most direct route between Christopher Circle and the cul-de-sac—unless I made a point of standing by the side of the road at the corner of our lot and waving them around like a traffic cop. It was too early to become a cul-de-sac curmudgeon—even one with a name as lovely as Something Suburban and Pretty. Such a role has to be earned over time. And we'd just moved in.

Meanwhile, I made the mistake of erecting our boys' swing set even before unpacking my own books. This meant that forty kids were swinging away in our backyard—morning, noon, and night—regardless of whether Owen and Adrian were out there. Others would flop on our lawn at the corner where Christopher Circle met the cul-de-sac—or leave their bikes there—as if it were a public park. I should have put a bench there for those who didn't like grass stains on their shorts. But then they would have expected Kool-Aid and cookies. They were very decent kids—midwestern kids devoid of accents, unconsciously causing Owen and Adrian to lose the trace of Virginia twang they'd brought with them—but there were just too many of them. All at once. All of the time.

Such an Ohio ambush, of course, was totally unexpected. It began the moment the moving van abandoned us that summer and continued for a year and a half until we moved again. I can remember driving down the street in our Nova with the family aboard, turning left onto the cul-de-sac, then left again into our driveway, with a pack of kids on bicycles gaining on us in the rearview mirror, trailing us right up to our automatic garage door, which I shut right in their bright and shining faces. Owen and Adrian, of course, were delighted with so many new friends, but it wasn't long before the incessant activity overwhelmed them, too.

Our two acres in southwest Virginia had afforded us 95 percent privacy, whereas our narrow northwest Ohio quarter-acre yielded but 5. We lived in a fishbowl at the center of a beehive in the middle of a pigeon coop, our house flanked by streets on the west and south and neighbors on the north and east. Thus we were happy when school began. Owen was starting third grade and Adrian was off to kindergarten. And the neighborhood calmed down during the day. We lived so close to campus that I biked to my office, returning in late afternoon just as the school bus released its pigeons. And the chaos resumed.

Ironically, I hadn't seen a single kid in the vicinity on the Saturday morning after my interview at the university, when I telephoned Elaine in Virginia before giving the realtor a down payment. It was noon, and all the kids were inside for lunch. We'd selected the house from photos and descriptions sent earlier. Like our home in Virginia, it had three bedrooms, a living room, kitchen, and dining room, plus a bonus—a family room with a fireplace and sliding glass doors to a wooden deck—a deck we promptly had roofed over and screened in as soon as the summer heat, thunderstorms, and standing water brought on a host of mosquitoes, making it impossible to be outside in our own backyard.

While the deck was under construction, Nils Riess dropped by to explain that everyone was chipping in to have the neighborhood fogged for mosquitoes. He lived on the cul-de-sac, the first home on the left behind ours, his side yard abutting our rear. A gregarious individual who appeared in local TV commercials, he was a chain-smoker who could have fogged the neighborhood himself by simply smoking outdoors. I'd already met his wife, Susan, an attractive woman who taught elementary school.

"Any children?" she'd called over the fence. Nils and Susan had two young daughters, a big shaggy dog, and a yard enclosed by a rail fence covered with a kind of chicken wire.

"Two boys!" I'd called back.

Susan shrugged. "We were hoping for girls!"

Nils worked at the university—he was head of the Theater Department—although he'd initially considered the ministry. "God's all an act, anyway," he said. Or something like that. Which endeared him to me immediately. For, as in Virginia, God was all over northwest Ohio—especially on billboards, which ranged from pro-life to anti-Halloween. Then there was the small sign at a rural crossroads a few miles south of us, fixed to the wall above a Pepsi machine outside a general store:

Thou shall not steal. Thou sins will find you out.
—God

With a postscript below God's signature:

Machine emptied daily.

In the bottom corner of that sign a symbol of a camera winked at the viewer, indicating that the premises were monitored by videotape. Thus prospective thieves received multiple warnings—from the Bible, God Himself (who'd dare fault His faulty usage?), and the ambiguous information that *something* was emptied daily (coins or cans of Pepsi?)—all while Big Brother was watching.

But the most egregious evidence of God we would encounter in northwest Ohio was a dining room wall in the house of a neighbor, an entire wall filled by a mural of *The Last Supper*. I'd grown up in Connecticut with an eight-by-ten-inch rendition of *The Last Supper* hung by my mother above the dining room table. But a wall-to-wall, floor-to-ceiling mural?

4

As Nils said, "God's all an act, anyway."

Or something like that.

Meanwhile, during that first hot and chaotic summer on Christopher Horseshoe, a hired tanker truck slipped into the neighborhood after dark to attack the mosquitoes. Minutes later a thick gray smoke billowed eerily through the trees like a ghost, leaving an oily stench that by morning had settled on the ground. It reminded me of the witches in *Macbeth*, which I'd be teaching that fall—*hover through the fog and filthy air*. This was before scientists learned how to mix natural pyrethrins with piperonyl butoxide for clean and efficient fogging. Instead, chemicals reminiscent of Agent Orange were unleashed into the atmosphere. Our only defense was to hunker down in our air-conditioned homes.

After the fogging, of course, the mosquitoes were as thick as ever, making us glad that we'd hired a local artisan to roof over and screen in our rear deck. But hey, we were the new kids on the block, happy to watch our money go up in smoke in the name of neighborhood solidarity.

Besides the deck and family room, our new ranch house had one other feature we'd never experienced before—a crawl space. Which is a literal description if there ever was one. The Great Black Swamp had seen to it that basements were a rarity in northwest Ohio—we would experience but one in our three Ohio homes, a basement that would teach us the meaning of "sump pump." Crawl spaces were the norm, and the one on Christopher Horseshoe was a novelty to me.

I went down there only once—through a trap door in a kitchen closet—crawling on hands and knees over a sharp bed of gravel while trying to run wiring for our computer to a back bedroom. Given that I'm six feet four inches tall, I kept bumping my head on the floor joists while cobwebs clotted my hair. It was dank and musty down there, and I should have worn gloves and jeans, because that bed of gravel left my hands and knees scraped and bleeding. Still, I had to be thankful for that crawl space.

"It's a great place to hide from tornados," the realtor had said.

Not to mention all those kids.

. . .

Soon after the fogging of our neighborhood, another chemical-laden tanker rolled up the street, turned onto the cul-de-sac, and pulled into our driveway. It was driven by a young man in his late teens. With the truck idling, the driver flipped through a clipboard, then hopped from the cab as if on a mission. Going straight to the rear of the truck, he began to unwind a thick hose, pulling it around to the front of the house.

"Whoa, there!" I said, banging out the front door. "Who are you?"

"I'm your ChemLawn man!" he announced brightly.

I'd forgotten about that. But the previous owner had warned me. He'd subscribed to ChemLawn—hence the lovely green carpet surrounding our house—and the service would continue unless I expressly stopped it.

"I want to expressly stop this service," I said. "We've just been fogged for mosquitoes. There are entirely too many chemicals on the ground. The kids are always jumping from the swings and rolling in the grass."

The young man looked expressly disappointed. You could tell that ChemLawn wasn't just his summer job—it was his career instead of college. He depended on polluting the atmosphere for a living. Still, I was proud of my steadfast refusal. This was the era of the greening of America—but not by ChemLawn—an era of growing environmental consciousness. And I didn't want to render my own kids unconscious by having them breathe chemicals all day. I thought I could battle the lawn on my own.

I was wrong, of course. And several weeks later, as if in spite, light-green blades of grass, larger than the rest in the dark-green lawn, began popping up out front—exactly the kind that are perfect for tucking between your thumbs to make a shrill whistle. So I plucked one and entertained the neighborhood kids by showing them how to do it. But I had an ulterior motive. I was hoping they'd rid my yard of those light-green blades by plucking them for whistles. Which they did—for a few days at least—as shrill whistling echoed around Christopher Horsehoe.

But the more those kids plucked and whistled, the more those light-green blades kept popping up. Finally, out of morbid curiosity, I let a few grow, just to see what would happen. What happened was, after a few days, those initial light-green shoots turned to three or four on a single stalk, looking like newly sprouted corn. But the corn in northwest Ohio had already sprouted in the spring and was now fifteen feet tall in the surrounding fields. So that stuff in the yard wasn't corn.

But what was it?

Before long those shoots reddened at the bottom and developed a shallow root structure. Then they got taller, sending a single shoot skyward with a narrow seed head, until the entire entity resembled a plant from a wheat field. When it was knee high I pulled up a stalk, took it to campus, and showed it to the head of the Biology Department.

"What you have there," he said, "is wild fescue."

Well, fesk YOU! I felt like saying—not to the head of the Biology Department, but to the plant itself. And to myself as well, I suppose, for having abandoned the ChemLawn service.

"We're raising kids," Elaine had to remind me. "Not chemicals."

She had a point. So I got into the habit of sitting out in the yard with a plastic bag and plucking stalk after stalk of wild fescue. Until fall came and it died out on its own. Leaving me with another problem.

Leaves.

. . .

Besides his ChemLawned lawn, the previous owner of our new home had been meticulous about a lot of things. The shrubs along the front of the house, for example, were neatly landscaped with thick mulch, underlined with a broad layer of black plastic.

I'd never seen that done before. Of course—under *my* care, at least—that subterranean black plastic simply absorbed the heat in summer, so that after a good rain, the weeds grew *on top of* the mulch. And the shrubs had to be weeded anyway.

The previous owner had also laced the gutters with porous plastic leaf-guards that arched up at roof level all around the house to encourage the leaves to join the weeds in the mulch below. We had oak leaves mainly, from a stand of enormous oaks in the northeast corner of the backyard. In the shade of which I'd reassembled the swing set. And in the fall, all of those leaves would, well, fall.

This had never been a problem in southwest Virginia, where the slope of our property had sent the gigantic leaves from our tulip poplar skittering into the surrounding woods on their own. I never once had to rake them. But on Christopher Horseshoe, by the end of October, we were ankle deep in crispy, crackling oak leaves.

And as soon as I started raking those leaves into piles, Owen and Adrian began jumping into them, requiring me to rake them into piles all over again while I debated what to do—with Owen and Adrian as well as those leaves.

After wrestling all that wild fescue into plastic bags for disposal, I couldn't face another such chore. So I borrowed Nils's apple cart—the kind you see in street market scenes in *The Godfather* films. It might have been a theater prop from one of Nils's university musicals, and I felt a bit retro in using it, but its capacity was greater than that of my wheelbarrow. Just perfect for piles of leaves.

When dumped into the Great Black Swamp at the end of the street, those leaves looked like so many brown caskets, having assumed the shape of the cart. Nils's apple cart had become a tumbrel from *Les Miserables,* used for trundling folks to the guillotine.

As for Owen and Adrian, I simply banished them from the yard while I worked, leaving them to their own devices. Which, of course, was a mistake.

Because as I was loading leaves into the tumbrel, the neighborhood grew noticeably quiet—as quiet as that fateful Saturday after my university interview. There was a slight chill in the air, high white clouds overhead, and a bit of dew beneath the crunching oak leaves. But something was up. It was too quiet. And when I wheeled those brown caskets to the end of the street, I learned the source of the silence.

Owen and Adrian and the flock of neighborhood pigeons had erected a plywood ramp over a few cement blocks and were flying their bicycles off the end of it right into the leaves—like Evel Knievel over the Grand Canyon. Worse yet, they were daring each other to lie beneath the end of that ramp while bikes flew over them. Owen and Adrian had graduated from Big Wheels to two-wheelers, although Adrian's still had training wheels, which was doubly dangerous.

Fesk you ALL! I felt like shouting.

But no words were necessary. At the approaching rumble of the tumbrel, the flock took off, abandoning their bikes for the safety of the Great Black Swamp, Owen and Adrian leading the way. So I dumped my leaves, dismantled the ramp, loaded the plywood and cinderblocks into the tumbrel, and headed home.

Where I found Owen and Adrian in the backyard raking the leaves into piles. Within range of the swing set.

Yard Wars of the Ohio Outback

Edifices Wrecked

The first victim of my northwest Ohio yard wars was a little critter we came to call "the skittery chipmunk." I would have left it alone if it had stayed outside, but it preferred the garage. How it got in there was a mystery. And once I solved it, there was nothing to do but execute the poor thing. For which Owen and Adrian threatened to report me to the SPCA.

It all started one Saturday after school began. We were driving home in the Nova, with the usual flock of kids on bicycles gaining on us in the rearview mirror—until we turned left onto the cul-de-sac, left again into our driveway, and shut the garage door in their bright and shining faces.

Then, as I got out of the car, a furry brown creature with black stripes on its back came skidding by me, its paws scrabbling furiously as it tried to turn by the wheelbarrow resting upright against the wall. Its attempt was as futile as it was comic—nails scratching the concrete as it slid on by like a creature in a Disney cartoon.

"Chipmunk!" I yelled. And that did it. Owen and Adrian tumbled out of the car and tore the garage apart trying to find the terrified interloper. Which by then, of course, had gained its footing and disappeared.

We saw it again, under similar circumstances, a few days later, and before long Owen and Adrian became quite fond of it, although they never saw it for more than a few seconds at a time. Elaine, not one for rodents, abstained from the enthusiasm. But she was touched by the boys' kind regard for it.

"A skittery chipmunk is better than a goldfish," she said. "You don't have to change its water."

One night, as I carried a bag of trash from the kitchen to a metal garbage can in the garage, I encountered the skittery chipmunk, startling it when I snapped on the light. The chipmunk froze, then panicked, scampering left and right before it got its bearings and headed for the wheelbarrow in a cartoonish cloud of dust.

The following morning I investigated, beginning out front beneath the garage windows. There, behind one of the shrubs, I found a hole through the mulch and black plastic—a hole that went deep below the foundation of the garage. The crawl space did not extend beyond the house itself. Had the skittery chipmunk chosen the crawl space, I would have let it live in peace. But as I said, it preferred the garage.

Little bits of white stuff lined that hole, and after I dug it out with my mattock, I realized what it was—crumbs of Styrofoam from the insulation between the cement foundation and the garage wall. Apparently that chipmunk liked the taste of Styrofoam, because it had chewed its way right through it, creating a tunnel wide enough for squirrels or skunks. Which, of course, wouldn't do.

Opening the garage door, I backed out the Nova, parked the wheelbarrow outside as well, and tore open the inside garage wall to reveal the skittery chipmunk's little den, which it accessed through a tiny crack at the bottom of the wallboard. Evidently it liked the taste of wallboard as much as Styrofoam. And mulch and black plastic to boot.

So I put a brick in front of the crack in the wallboard and went back out front, where I rammed a few more bricks into that chipmunk's tunnel, tamping them firm with the butt end of a heavy pike. Then I replaced the dirt, cut up a black plastic bag, covered it with mulch, and dusted my hands with satisfaction.

"I saw the skittery chipmunk!" Adrian said a few days later. "When I put my bike in the garage!" He was proud of himself—for having seen the chipmunk as well as riding his bike without training wheels.

"We left it peanut butter," Owen added. "It's our pet!"

Next morning, checking in the garage behind the wheelbarrow, I found my brick pushed away from the crack in the wallboard. And what I found out front was simply amazing. It looked like a mini-bomb had exploded behind the bush beneath the garage window. Bricks had been tossed aside willy-nilly, the earth and mulch and plastic in humps and bumps.

Goddam sunnuvabitch chipmunk!

It was war, of course. Which called for heavy artillery—in the form of a brand-new rattrap purchased at Furrows over in Lima, the local equivalent of 84 Lumber. I had considered a mousetrap at first but then thought the better of it. If the skittery chipmunk could handle bricks, it would laugh at a mousetrap. But a rattrap scared even me. It took all of my strength to set it after I'd laced its stiff brass trigger with peanut butter.

In the middle of the night I heard that trap go off with a *crack!* And first thing in the morning, as soon as Owen and Adrian had caught the bus for school, I quietly disposed of the limp corpse, the black stripes on its back perfectly perpendicular to the sharp crease in its neck. Then I patched up the garage wall, inside and out.

"Don't look at me like that," I said to Elaine as I walked into the kitchen, dusting my hands with satisfaction. "We're raising children, not chipmunks."

. . .

The local artisan who roofed over and screened in our deck was a short, swarthy handyman by the name of Jim Massillo. He rapidly became our go-to guy for all projects beyond my own shoemaker abilities. At our third home in northwest Ohio, Jim would cut a window into a bedroom wall, replace a leaky toilet, refloor two bathrooms, install a shower stall, and reshingle the roof. He'd earned our confidence with the dandy job he'd done roofing over and screening in our deck on Christopher Circle—complete with a screen door that closed itself quietly whenever Owen and Adrian banged their way outside.

Neatness was Jim's signature. When he finished a job, you couldn't tell that he'd been there. But his business card needed remodeling. In addition to his name and contact information, it sported a catchphrase: "Tasteful Edifices Erected."

You could tell Jim was proud of that phrase by the way he waited for a reaction when he handed me his card not long after we'd moved in.

"Well," I said finally, "we're in need of a tasteful edifice, so you must be the man for the job." Had I attempted to roof over and screen in that deck, it would have been a disaster. "My calling card," I said, "is Edifices Wrecked."

I'd be teaching *Oedipus Rex* that fall, along with *Macbeth* and other classics in my Great Works course. But the literary allusion was lost on Jim. Literature was not his thing. Lumber was, although he'd built a house "on spec" and lost his shirt. Hence his need for any-and-all odd jobs.

So we signed him up for a tasteful edifice. And his roofed-over, screened-in deck was a thing of beauty. Building it around the original deck flooring, Jim salvaged the excess lumber—a series of two-by-fours and narrow vertical railings—for a play fort I promised to build for Owen and Adrian. They wanted something high so they could hide from the neighborhood pigeons. They weren't allowed in the crawl space.

But first I had to resurrect their basketball hoop. Which only embarrassed them. Who wants the only backboard in northwest Ohio made from leftover boards? The other kids had nifty white fiberglass backboards. But I'd trucked that homemade backboard all the way from southwest Virginia with the intention of bolting it to the triangular peak above the garage door. Which I did after raking the leaves in the fall. And our concrete driveway provided a perfectly flat basketball court.

But shooting hoops out there became challenging. As soon as the basketball slapped the driveway, the pigeons descended. It was hard to play basketball with twenty kids on a side. So Owen and Adrian eagerly awaited their play-fort hideaway, which I erected in the far corner of the yard beneath the stand of oak trees that shaded the swing set.

But the location was a mistake. The oak trees had littered the ground with slippery acorns that I kept slipping on. It was like trying to work on a dance floor full of marbles.

"Goddam sunnuvabitch . . . !"

Yet those acorns had one salutary effect. The more I cursed them, the more the pigeons kept their distance.

I had a literal leg up on this play-fort project—a sixteen-foot four-inch-square post that had supported the boys' backboard in southwest Virginia. It had made the move to Ohio along with the backboard. I purchased three more exactly like it at Furrows and set to work with my post-hole digger. But I had to dig a dozen holes before I got four deep enough for the four-stilt foundation my design called for. Because I kept striking obstructions.

Goddam . . . roots!

I had to whack my way through them with a fireman's axe I'd bought after a severe ice storm in Virginia. But eventually four tall posts rose into the sky, joined by two-by-fours eight feet up to serve as joists for the plywood floor. Four feet higher I nailed another round of two-by-fours for the vertical railings Jim had salvaged from the deck. This made the fort look like a jail cell, so I enclosed it with plywood on the west and north sides—from whence came the weather—and covered the whole thing with a plywood roof.

"All in all," Elaine said, greeting me with Gatorade, "it's a rather tasteful edifice."

A ladder up the east side completed the project, and Owen and Adrian scrambled aloft before I'd put my tools away.

"Sorry!" they yelled to the pigeons flocking below. "There's only room for *two* up here!"

Like Jim Massillo, I cleaned up carefully, raking up the root chips that had flown all over the place and adding them to the mulch out front, so you couldn't even tell I'd been there. A family of squirrels was busily at work as well, cleaning up the acorns I hadn't trampled underfoot. They'd erected a nest high up in the oaks—like a large brown shopping bag full of sticks and leaves—in preparation for winter. We enjoyed a symbiotic relationship. They cleaned the yard of acorns, and I let them live—unlike their destructive cousin, the skittery chipmunk.

But by spring I'd be cursing those squirrels as well.

Which is the next time I saw Jim Massillo, parachuting into the center of campus at the conclusion of a university picnic after leaping from a small plane that had taken off from a nearby pasture. Skydiving was Jim's passion (one of my students would write a feature article about him for the campus paper), and a decade later Jim would die that way, suffering a heart attack as he descended, floating peace-fully from heaven only to turn around and go right back up, to that Stately Mansion in the sky.

One of the most tasteful edifices ever erected, to hear the locals tell it.

. . .

Before we could go to that university picnic in the spring, however, we had to survive the winter. Which proved difficult, given two un-expected events. The first was less serious than the second, but it ir-ritated me more because it sparked yet another yard war.

It happened after a major December snowstorm, our first experi-ence of snow in Ohio. It was rather pretty, actually—the snow de-scending peacefully throughout the day and night, accumulating to a depth of two feet and coating the branches of all trees as in a fairy tale. School was canceled, of course, and when the sun came out all the pigeons appeared, filling the sky with snowballs as the trucks plowed the roads.

It was the plowing of the roads that set me off.

"What's all that dark stuff along the edge of the yard?" Elaine asked, looking out front through the living room window.

"Don't know," I said. "I'll go have a look."

So I put on my boots and ski jacket and went out.

That dark stuff, as it turned out, was turf from our yard—rolled up like so many throw rugs by the guy who'd plowed Christopher Circle. He'd set his plow too low and lost sight of the edge of the road, which, as I said, had no curb. This put him two feet into our yard. By the time he'd turned left onto the cul-de-sac, he'd already rolled up twenty yards of turf, adding another ten before he reached our driveway. But those turf rolls were hardly neat. Large chunks of sod had flown all over the place, littering the yard like large divots on a golf course.

And who was going to replace all those divots? Me, as it turned out.

. . . *sunnuvabitch snowplow!*

As the snowplow driver reached our driveway, he must have seen in the rearview mirror the mess he was making. Because he suddenly veered to the right, leaving Nils's yard unscathed. He didn't stop, of course, but continued on his way.

So I trudged next door, catching Nils in a swirl of morning cigarette smoke, to ask if he knew the snowplow driver. Ironically, the name he offered—which I no longer recall—reflected a lack of awareness. Something like Dunce or Fluke. But the local phone book listed a hundred Flukes and Dunces, all related by their lack of intelligence.

"Hello," I began politely with my very first call. "Is Mr. Dunce there?"

"Which Dunce you want?"

"The one that does the plowing."

"Corn or soybeans?"

"*Snow*plowing!"

"Ain't nobuddy like that here."

After half a dozen conversations like this, I gave up. I didn't want to start a local feud between the Dunces and the Flukes. With me right in the middle. Instead, I opened the garage door and went out with my wheelbarrow to pick up the broken pieces of my own yard, stacking them between the bushes out front until I could fit them back into the dark scars along the edge of the road, which I did when the snow melted a few weeks later. It was like putting together a puzzle with pieces missing. And the yard looked like hell.

The second event that winter occurred at 11:47 on a Friday morning at the end of January. The first class I taught wasn't until two in the afternoon, so I was still at home, at my computer in the master bedroom, when the house suddenly shuddered. It was the kind of involuntary shudder I'd often experienced while taking a leak. But I hadn't been taking a leak. It was the house that had shuddered— from the master bedroom all the way to the garage. And then, just as suddenly, all was quiet.

"What the hell was that?" I called to Elaine. But Elaine had gone shopping in her Merry Monza, a car so light on its feet that it could barely feel the pavement, let alone an earthquake. Which was all over the news that evening.

Ohio had suffered an earthquake that measured 5 on the Richter scale. It'd been felt in eleven states, plus the District of Columbia and Ontario. The epicenter, just east of Cleveland, was the nearest ever to a power plant in the United States.

But early rumors of death and destruction proved false. Seventeen people were treated for injuries near the epicenter, but only two were a direct result of the quake. A woman was bruised by a falling ceiling tile in a shopping mall, and a child received a minor cut from a broken window. Others were treated for anxiety, or the effects of cold weather, after being evacuated from buildings suspected of damage.

Property damage was minor as well. Merchandise fell from store shelves, plaster walls cracked, and windows broke. One chimney toppled, while others sustained cracks or pulled away from attached structures. Students were sent home so school buildings could be inspected, but not in our neck of the woods. A few people reported that their well water had changed color. Others reported a change in its taste. Some wells went dry while others increased their flow.

People interviewed near the epicenter reported a variety of reactions. One thought a furnace had exploded. Another was convinced a truck had rammed her building. More fanciful interpretations included the recent aftershock of the explosion of the space shuttle Challenger and a nuclear attack on New York City.

So much for edifices wrecked.

I would have said it felt like taking a leak.

Made in Ada

The NFL Ball

Football-shaped nameplates mark the executive parking spaces at the Wilson Sporting Goods factory in Ada, Ohio. Inside the white cinder-block building a poster of Joe Theismann adorns the paneled waiting room wall. Back issues of *Sports Illustrated* dominate the magazines on the coffee table. I sign in with the receptionist and moments later am greeted by Steve Zuercher, the production superintendent, for a tour of the premises to see how the official NFL ball—the one that Joe Theismann is about to pass in that poster on the wall, the football known the world over—is made right here in Ada.

"Are footballs really pigskin?" I ask Steve Zuercher.

"That's a myth," he says. "They say the early ball was a pig's bladder covered with cowhide. But I've never seen one."

Joe Horrigan, director of research information at the Pro Football Hall of Fame in Canton, agrees. "There is no historical basis for the football as a pigskin," he says. "Legend dates the ball to England in the sixteen hundreds, when field hands played soccer using stuffed animal bladders, most likely from a cow or goat."

"A myth," Steve Zuercher says again. He has just returned from an equipment show in Atlanta, a trip he makes annually to view the latest sewing machines, laces, needles, threads—whatever might improve the operation in Ada. The show is hosted by the apparel industry, with displays by the same vendors that do business with Wilson. Zuercher is excited about one vendor he saw that gave a demonstration of modular production. The workers were making garments, but the process could be applied to making footballs.

"Sounds like it's gonna be a good concept," Zuercher says. "It's where you have a group of five to ten people do the complete product—all the people can do all the jobs involved—instead of an assembly line like we have here. Modular production increases quality and gives a group incentive. It just might be the way to go."

Other new ideas, like the computerized floor tracking system he saw, can be worked out in less time, say six to twelve months. The assembly line employees in Ada are on piecework. They keep track of what they turn out by attaching tickets as they proceed. But now there's a computerized bar-coding system that checks out work like groceries in a supermarket. It will help with inventory, too. Zuercher has to determine if it's worth the time and effort to convert.

But he saw one machine in Atlanta that could be used in Ada right away. It would put a pricing barcode on each finished ball, so the retailer could put it directly on the shelf. At present a plastic bar-coded tag—which the customer has to cut off—is tied to the laces of each ball by hand.

"Next year when we go to Atlanta all this stuff will be updated," Zuercher says. "There'll be new stamping and splitting and cutting machines. But we have to keep up. You never want to get complacent."

The Wilson factory is in its second year of a rolling five-year contract for exclusive production of the NFL ball. It also produces 88 percent of all high school and college footballs. The closest competitors are Rawlings and Spaulding.

What gives Wilson the edge? "Our people," Zuercher says without hesitation. "They're the best. In quality and experience. Come on. I'll show you."

But before we can get back into the factory, a phone call interrupts, so I am turned over to Dick Price, the production supervisor, who hands me a pair of safety glasses and leads the way to the shop.

Hanging overhead by the time cards in the hallway of the employees' entrance is an enormous football, about ten times regulation size. As I gawk at it, the hum of machinery fills my ears, a whirring noise punctuated by what sounds like riveting, then louder bursts that sound like a jackhammer, then blasts of air like the brakes on a bus.

"The founder of this business," Dick Price explains, "was Bill Sonnett Sr. He brought the company to Ada from Cincinnati in 1938. It was originally the Ohio-Kentucky Manufacturing Company. Sonnett was looking for a rural community, and somebody told him about Ada—nice quiet area, college town—it was ideal. Wilson bought him out in 1955."

Dick Price has worked at Wilson's for twenty-six years. His wife, Peggy, who runs the die-out machine that punches lace holes, has been here twenty-three years. Their daughter, Michele Price Smith, runs the machine that paints white stripes on the college and high school balls. She's been here eleven years. The dedication of the Prices is typical. More than 500 employee family members enjoyed the recent company picnic. You'd never guess that the Wilson Company is a union shop. Management speaks highly of labor, and labor speaks highly of management.

The high-ceilinged work area at the Ada plant is roughly the size and shape of a football field. We enter by the home team's bench. The stock room is the open area in the end zone to our far left. Four parallel lines of work stations run from left to right straight up the field, fed by conveyor belts that carry the work to 110 individuals. Three men in the stock room tend the belts, loading and unloading plastic bins the size of large laundry baskets. Larger bins—trucks on wheels—are pushed to work stations along the sidelines to cart off the finished balls. The plant is warm and clean, and the workers are dressed comfortably in jeans, khakis, and short-sleeved shirts.

But what strikes you immediately is the activity—the more than one hundred workers intent on their jobs, moving at a pace that is almost frantic. The place jumps with disciplined energy, the motions quick, animated, repetitive.

"We make 20,000 to 25,000 balls a week," Dick Price says matter-of-factly. "It's enough to make you dizzy."

The noise grows louder. The "riveting" is from the sewing machines, durable German-made industrial versions of the old Singer you might have at home. The "jackhammers" are actually pounders, machines that soften the tough leather seams of the football. These machines, as well as those that cut, stamp, and punch the leather, look like large drill presses. They operate under hydraulic pressure, hence the frequent blasts of air. Beyond them are other worktables where crucial steps in the production are done by hand.

"It all begins here," Dick Price continues. We are in the stock room, at a table piled high with steer hides. The leather comes from the stockyards near Chicago. Each hide is about six feet square, scalloped along the edges where it was cut above the animal's legs and again at the neck and rump. The thinner leather lies to the outside. It's used for the lesser grades of retail footballs. The best leather lies along the backbone. This is reserved for the NFL ball.

Natural leather is beige in color, but the hides on the table have been dyed and pebbled at the tannery. The dye makes the ball the reddish-brown color you see on TV. The pebbling produces the nubbled texture that makes it easier to grip. The Wilson operation consumes forty to fifty thousand square feet of leather a week—ten times as much as its largest competitor. It takes two square feet of leather to make a single ball.

"The cutters have the real responsibility," Dick Price says as we start down the line. "Leather is expensive. They have to avoid waste."

The cutters work a flat football-shaped die across the steer hide, applying pressure from their hydraulic drill presses, stamping out leather panels like cookies out of dough. Each ball consists of four such panels. Quality control workers check the cutting die weekly to make sure its dimensions haven't changed. The finished ball must be at least eleven inches long, with a small circumference of twenty-one inches and a long circumference of twenty-eight. The NFL allows tolerances on these dimensions from one-quarter to half an inch, because leather has a tendency to change with the weather.

The football-shaped panels are then color-matched by sight. Some are darker than others. Being a natural material, leather has its inconsistencies, so the dye doesn't always take evenly at the tannery. The matched panels are marked, stacked in fours beside the cutting machine, and sent to the stamper, who, applying heat as well as hydraulic pressure, brands the Wilson logo into the leather along with the NFL insignia and any autographs or information that the NFL wants to place there. For the Super Bowl, the names of the competing teams are added to each ball in a special design. Once ink was used, but today the gleaming logos are pressed in with colored foil.

The stamped panels are then sent to the splitter, who feeds them through a machine with rollers—rather like a washing machine ringer—containing a thin horizontal blade. They come out as split grain. The wrinkled matter that drops to the floor from beneath the pebbled surface is discarded at the landfill, although some manufacturers sell it as fertilizer. Split-grain leather is used in retail products such as billfolds and jackets. Wilson uses it for the lesser-grade footballs. The NFL and college balls are top grain, missing the full force of the splitter's blade.

At this point the panels are weighed, the first of three quality-control weight checks. The finished NFL product—spiraling through the air toward some receiver's outstretched hands—must weigh between fourteen and fifteen ounces.

"These are preliminary steps," Dick Price explains. I'm already beginning to feel cut, stamped, and split by the noise. He has to shout to be heard. "The real strength of the ball is not in the leather. Leather likes to stretch. It's the lining that keeps the ball in shape. We used to use cotton liners, but now we use man-made nylon fabric. It's preshrunk and three-ply. There's no way it can change shape."

We move to the next station, where a woman is sewing linings to the underside of the panels. The white linings, also football-shaped, resemble stiff gauze or muslin. The sewing machines on the assembly lines can run at five thousand revolutions per minute and produce up to eighteen stitches per second. At that speed the needle smokes against the leather, cooling just enough as the operator stops to snip the thread and pick up the next piece. None of the sewing is freehand. The linings are placed flat against the panels then held against a gauge and rotated as the needle runs the stitch. The operator has to place the work correctly and the machine does the rest.

For the lesser-grade balls nylon thread is used, and the machine runs a continuous chain stitch. But for the NFL ball—"our Cadillac," Dick Price says—a braided Dacron thread is used with a lock stitch. With each stitch locked automatically in place, it's impossible for the thread to unravel.

"Ninety percent of our employees are women," Dick Price notes.

"They're a lot more adept at sewing and lacing. But there are certain jobs they're just not strong enough to do. You'll see those later."

A large elderly man in a baseball cap passes by. "That's Barney Shields, the maintenance supervisor," Dick Price says. "He's our oldest employee. Worked here longer than anybody. I don't know what we're going to do when he retires. Barney put in all the plumbing and wiring. He's modified by hand most of the machinery we've got. He's a carpenter, a self-taught engineer—he's got this whole plant stored in his head."

Leaving the assembly line momentarily, we catch up to Barney Shields at the far end of the shop, where a few employees are taking a coffee break. At sixty-seven, Barney is as talkative as he is indispensable.

"I've been workin' for this outfit since February 28, 1942," he says proudly. "I started uptown—we had another plant in those days— turnin' baseball gloves at twenty-seven and one-half cents an hour. I've been a receiving clerk, a shipping clerk, a cutter. Done all the jobs except sewin' and lacin'. I came up through the ranks the hard way. Bill Sonnet Sr. was my boss. He was quite a guy. If he ever had somethin' to say to you, he said it with a smile. But if you put a pipe down the wall, it'd better be perpendicular!"

"Any time we need anything around here," Dick Price chips in, "all we do is say, 'Hey, Barney!' He's made the bladder tables, the turning tables, the striping tables, the roll pounder. Our competitors would love to see some of Barney's inventions, but we don't allow photographs. The improvements aren't patented."

Barney Shields has no plans to retire—"They'd only be callin' me back anyway for one thing or another"—so for the time being his expertise is assured. But his ingenuity doesn't always make him happy. He's got an idea now for adapting a machine that would put a lot of employees out of work. The possibility bothers him, so he's leaving the idea "on the back burner."

A self-educated man, Barney Shields is an inspiration. In a world driven by high technology, it's refreshing to know that some things— like the NFL ball—are a product of practical experience, that quality depends on craftsmanship. What the artisans of Ada produce, in effect, is a bona fide work of art.

I shake hands with Barney Shields and follow Dick Price back to the assembly line to watch the lined panels sewn together to make a football. And what I see next amazes me.

Picture two football-shaped panels, one stamped *Wilson* and the other stamped *NFL*. These are held flat together for stitching along the top edge, the white linings facing out and the logos facing in. The bottom two panels are similarly joined, lining out, pebbled grain to pebbled grain. Then, when the two half-sections are sewn together, the deflated ball is actually *inside out*. At this point it looks like the stiff, dry pith of some exotic, elongated fruit.

Given the thickness of full-grain leather and the stiff edges left by the cutter, the seams produced when the panels are sewn together are cumbersome and sharp. The ball is made inside out so that the seams can be pounded smooth. Otherwise, they would make the air bladder, inserted later, go flat. This *carcass*—as the ball is called at this point—will eventually be "turned," leaving the seams on the inside. It will be turned right-side out *by hand*.

Before that can be done, however, several steps intervene. Sixteen lace holes—eight to each side of the top seam—are punched into the leather, and an opening is created through which the bladder will be inserted. An elongated oval flap is sewn to each side of the opening to protect the bladder from the laces. In addition, a hole is punched for the valve on the bladder. Then the ball is sent to the pounders.

The Wilson factory uses two types of pounders—a half-section roll pounder that Barney Shields invented and a four-section pounder for the inside-out ball. Dick Price reminds me that films and photographs of the former are prohibited. And since a thousand words can make a picture, I focus my attention on the latter, a drill press type of machine that sounds like a jackhammer and pounds like one. The operator works the inside-out carcass down over a mushroom-shaped pounding head through the opening where the laces will go. Then he works the seams of the ball around the head while the machine applies a blunt hammerlike tool from above. The rapid-fire pounding is repeated until the seams are soft and smooth. Then the carcass is tossed into a basket and the conveyor belt takes them up the line to the turning tables.

The turning operation requires brute strength, so the turners are all men. Each worktable consists of a pounding head, where the seams are pounded again briefly with a mallet, and an upright turning bar on which the carcass is wrestled right-side out. Bolted upright, the turning bar resembles the floor shift of a pickup truck. One of the turners, Charlie Moore, has been working at Wilson's for twenty-five years. He is slightly built but wiry, with wrists and forearms as tough as the full-grain leather he handles. With quick, jerky movements he puts the full weight of his body behind each ball, twisting the carcass about the turning bar. At times he seems to be break dancing, at times doing ballet. When he's done, the carcass is right-side out, looking at last like a football.

"Charlie's career was extended ten years by that steam box there," Dick Price says. "That's another one of Barney Shield's inventions. The men discovered it was easier to turn footballs in summer because the heat and humidity soften the leather. So they talked with Barney and he came up with that box."

The steam box on the corner of Charlie Moore's table is like a kiln, about the size of a microwave oven. Each carcass is put in for a few seconds and comes out steaming. Charlie Moore hands me one. It feels hot, moist, and pliable.

"The steam takes the physical strain out of the ball," he explains. "It softens the lining. It saves my hands. That steam box is a big deal on this assembly line."

Charlie Moore turns between 500 and 800 footballs a day—a strenuous effort. I ask him what he thinks about while working.

"Not much," he admits. "You can't stand and daydream. You gotta concentrate and watch what you're doing. You gotta keep the seams straight. Especially where they come together at the end of the ball."

He takes the carcass from me and slips it over the turning bar, and I follow Dick Price on up the line.

Women at the next station are inserting bladders into each carcass. The bladders for the NFL ball are made of butyl, the same synthetic rubber used in inner tubes and tires. The lesser-grade footballs receive a bladder of urethane. Large fans blow across the bladder tables, drying the special glue that attaches the valve to each bladder. Once the bladder is inserted into the carcass, the operator pushes a pedal and a regulator inflates the ball to four pounds of pressure. Though still underinflated, it is easier to handle for the women who do the lacing.

Michelle Burkett, at the next station, has been lacing footballs at the Wilson factory for thirteen years. Bent over the ball in her lap, she digs at it furiously. It looks like she's sewing up a stuffed turkey. Three fingers on each hand are wrapped with thick rings of adhesive tape, and her wrists are bound with elastic bandages for support. She uses an awl to push the two twenty-nine-inch white laces through the holes at the top of the ball, working one lace up, the other back down. She laces three hundred footballs a day.

"The laces are made to look like leather," Dick Price explains, "but leather laces dry and crack. For the NFL ball we use a waterproof latex cover over a nylon filler. Actually, it's the stitching—not the lacing—that holds the ball together. As hard as it's kicked in the NFL, not one ball has ever come apart."

Michelle Burkett reaches for a pair of scissors, snips the lacing clean, and tosses the ball into the basket.

"Michelle's left-handed," Dick Price continues. "We almost didn't hire her, because the lacing pattern is designed to come to the right. She had to train herself, and she's done so well we now have three lefties on the line."

"I had a lot of pain in my right hand when I started," Michelle admits. "I don't think they knew I was left-handed. I took the whole end of my thumb off several times—not with the awl but with the scissors. Sometimes I look like I've been in a war zone."

As we move on, I ask Dick Price about job-related injuries.

"There aren't many," he says. "Oh, every once in a while somebody will put a needle through their finger and we'll have to take 'em to a local doctor and get it out. But it never gets more serious than that."

We follow the laced footballs to the next station, where they are put into a large cylinder that is molded inside to the shape of a football. Here, to stretch out the kinks, the balls are quickly inflated to eighty pounds of air, then the pressure is dropped to thirteen pounds, the specified NFL pressure.

Since there are no stripes on the NFL ball—"The stadium lighting is so sophisticated there's no need," Dick Price says—we skip the next station, where a machine paints stripes on the college and high school balls.

The inspection station lies ahead. Quality control. But en route we pass a table that makes me blink. It is piled high with "gimmick" products—footballs made of imitation crocodile skin, elephant skin, ostrich skin. Gaudy and tacky, they are nonetheless authentic footballs.

"We even have horned toad footballs," Dick Price says. "And several years ago we made a ball that was completely orange. For a while it was our top seller. You never know what people will go for."

On this table, too, are the autographed footballs you can buy at the stadium, the players' signatures transferred by silk screen. "We put anything on the football the customer wants," Dick Price says. "We've made some with the picture of a cow on them and some with ice cream sundaes. A special logo is designed for the Super Bowl."

That's when things get hectic. Eight thousand new footballs are made for the Super Bowl—100 game balls, 200 practice balls, and 7,000 balls for promotion and retail. Production begins on Sunday afternoon, as soon as the playoffs end. The competing teams begin practice on Tuesday afternoon, and the new balls—shipped *Tuesday morning*—are there. After such a spirited effort, as Wilson comptroller Greg Miller, attests, "You get a warm feeling when you see that ball on your television screen."

We reach the inspection tables and Dick Price tosses me a new ball. "This is it," he says. "Our Cadillac." It is shiny and slippery and exciting to hold. I cock it in my arm like Joe Theismann in that poster on the waiting room wall.

"The women at this station weigh the finished ball once again," Dick Price continues. "They check the length and diameter. They also do cosmetic checks, straightening the laces and clipping threads. Then the balls are sorted. Only 20 percent will qualify as NFL game balls. They are as perfect as footballs can be. The next best are sold retail. You can buy one yourself at any good sporting goods store for about $50. Balls with blemishes—blems—are sold as seconds."

At the packing area, as a courtesy to store owners, a theft-proof nylon tie for the price tag is attached through the laces. Then the retail balls are placed in an open-face box—an attractive orange display carrier marked Wilson—because customers like to be able to touch the ball in the store. Those destined for the NFL are packed in plastic bags within a simpler box. To prevent theft, there are no identifiable markings on the large packing boxes that carry the balls by the hundreds from the plant.

"There you have it," Dick Price says. We are at the employees' entrance once again, the home team's bench.

I look back along the assembly line. It is 11:00 A.M. We began our tour at nine. The frantic pace has not lessened, the machinery still whirs—the riveting, the pounding, the air brakes. The herky-jerky turners at their tables.

Kickoff time is 6:00 A.M. daily at the Wilson plant in Ada, sending the NFL ball your way.

Yard Wars of the Ohio Outback

Sacre Bleu!

Our first spring in northwest Ohio brought with it such a series of plagues that it seemed like we'd bought our new place from Job himself.

It began innocently enough, when I went outside to mow the lawn in the merry month of May. But a stiff breeze picked up and it started snowing! The temperature was seventy-five, the sky was light blue, and it was suddenly snowing a funny kind of snow—as if Mother Nature was hosting a gigantic pillow fight. Sticky, white, fluffy stuff filled the air, dancing up and down in the breeze before eventually settling quietly all over Christopher Circle, the cul-de-sac, lawns, rooftops—everything. I'd never seen anything like it. I began looking for Mr. Dunce-Fluke with his plow.

"What the hell *is* that stuff?" I called over the fence to Nils, who, wrapped as he was in a perpetual cloud of cigarette smoke, seemed oblivious.

"What stuff?" he called back.

"The . . . snow!"

"Oh. That's just the cottonwoods doin' their thing."

A mighty contingent of cottonwood trees, as it turned out, thrived in the remnants of the Great Black Swamp—and in many backyards of the neighborhood—although our yard sported only oaks. When these cottonwoods bloomed or shed or "did their thing" in the spring, they laced the air with incredibly light white seeds that coated the grass and clogged the lawn mower, forcing me to rake the yard before I could mow. It was so stunning that I called to Elaine through an open window to come out and witness the phenomenon.

"Only in northwest Ohio," she said, "can you shovel snow and rake it, too."

I'd had no experience with cottonwoods whatsoever, somehow associating them with those John Wayne movies in which a lonesome cowpoke says "I'm gonna get me a little spread down by the bend in the river where the cottonwoods grow." And rake snow.

The plague of the cottonwoods lasted for a week or two, preventing me from mowing the lawn. The white stuff clogged the Lawn Boy, and trying to dispose of it after raking was like trying to fill a plastic garbage bag with cotton candy.

In contrast, the second plague lasted longer and was noisier—a loud drone that started suddenly one morning and ended weeks later, as if Mother Nature was making a phone call with a colossally bad connection. Yet we still got the message.

"What the hell's that noise?" I called over the fence to Nils, who, wrapped as he was in a perpetual cloud of cigarette smoke, seemed oblivious.

"What noise?" he said.

"That goddam sunnuvabitch hum!"

"Oh. That noise. Sounds like the seventeen-year cicadas are back."

And they were. With a vengeance. Which is the only way, I suppose, that you *can* come back if you come back only once every seventeen years. We would witness the plague again before the end of our second decade in Ohio, but this was our very first.

"The life cycle of the seventeen-year cicada," the head of the Biology Department told me, "is among the most remarkable of any insect. It begins with an egg deposited within the bark of a tree. When it hatches, it crawls or falls to the ground, where it burrows in and remains for the next seventeen years feeding on roots and plant matter."

"And now?"

"Now the nymphs are digging their way out and attaching themselves to trees while they molt into adults, complete with wings. Then they start courting and mating."

So what we were hearing was a bunch of horny grasshoppers.

"The adults," he continued, "live for only a short time, so the females hurry to lay their eggs. Then the cycle begins all over again."

As the annoying noise rose to the heavens, the ground became coated with the translucent exoskeletons of giant grasshoppers, which, after raking snow, I wasn't about to rake up. The journalists waxed poetic, of course, calling the cicadas "a symphony of drones." They compared it to *Symphonie Fantastique*—the sublimation of Hector Berlioz's obsession with the unattainable woman. Meanwhile, I exorcised the little demons with the Lawn Boy, chewing up and spitting out their symphonic corpses.

During the molting, Jack Nicklaus's Memorial Tournament was under way down in Dublin, Ohio. I watched it on TV, empathizing with the frustrated pro golfers who, time and again, had to brush cicadas from the line of their putts. Cicadas littered the greens, while microphones around the course caught their droning. The commentators had to compete with it as well, and it prompted a phone call to Christopher Circle from my older brother in Connecticut. We'd grown up playing golf together, following the pros, and he, of course, was watching the tournament on TV too.

"What the hell's that noise?" he wanted to know.

"What noise?" I said.

"That goddam sunnuvabitch hum!"

"Oh. *That* noise. That's just the cicadas doin' their thing."

. . .

The third plague that spring was caused by the same squirrels I'd praised in the fall for clearing the backyard of acorns. But as everyone knows, what goes up must come down.

In this case, what went up were acorns and what came down were fragments of shells, covering the lawn like shards of glass. The large baglike squirrels' nest was still up there in the tallest oak tree. Worse yet, two or three little gray squirrels were now running around with the big ones, romping among the branches overhanging the play-fort and swing set, all of them pausing to perch every so often with a nut in their paws, chomping away while their sharp crumbs fell to earth.

Owen and Adrian complained. They loved to run barefoot on the soft lawn in the back yard, but now it was a field of shrapnel, making them hop lightly between the swing set and play-fort.

"Wear your sneakers," I told them. "I'll take care of this."

"You won't hurt them, will you?" Owen said.

"The little ones remind me of the skittery chipmunk!" Adrian said.

I promised I'd be gentle, lest they report me to the SPCA.

But the first skirmish in this particular battle wasn't even worthy of the name. I waited until Owen and Adrian's bus left for school, then took a hardball from Owen's baseball glove and heaved it as high as I could overhead, never once hitting the nest. All that ball did was knock about in the branches and fall right back to me. As with the acorns, I realized, what goes up must come down. Heaving that baseball, however, set the squirrels a-chattering. But they settled down just as quickly—as quickly as it took my arm to tire after half a dozen throws.

That nest, I now knew, wasn't going anywhere. It was too high to reach even with my extension ladder, and the highest branches of that oak were too dangerous to climb. I needed a new strategy, which my father, in an uncanny coincidence, soon provided.

He'd recently installed a trellis-cum-bird feeder back home in Connecticut. Squirrels had been ravaging that feeder, he told me on the phone, taking all the birdseed. So he'd sent away for a squirrel trap and disposed of them, taking them for a ride and releasing them out in the country.

"I'll ship it to you," he said. Which he did, by UPS. The squirrel trap arrived a few days later in a long rectangular box. Complete with instructions in French: "Votre première étape pour atraper votre écureuil gris est d'effectuer un petit travail révélateur. Trouver le chemin que l'écureuil utilize à votre traçage ou où jamais il ne devrait pas être."

Great. I'd spent a summer in France when I was single, at which time I was more interested in *chaser les femmes* than *atraper votre écureuil gris.* My father had ordered the squirrel trap from Maine or Canada and set it up without even reading the directions. A retired engineer, he just looked at that trap and knew how it worked. Whereas I headed for the French dictionary tucked away with the other books I hadn't unpacked since moving in. Because I'd set up the swing set. After which the Ohio yard wars had begun in earnest and hadn't ceased.

The squirrel trap was a wire cage in the shape of a trapezoid, with a wire handle on top for convenient carrying about. The slanted ends of the trapezoid flipped up and out from the base—at which point the wire cage resembled a covered bridge—so a squirrel could enter from either end. But as soon as the *écureuil gris* touched the small bait pan in the center—a hair-trigger mechanism as finicky as a mousetrap—those slanted ends collapsed with a bang, and what seemed to be a covered bridge with a tasty snack in the middle transformed itself into a trapezoidal wire cage, a panicked squirrel scurrying back and forth within.

After struggling with the French instructions for an hour or so, I gave up and decided to wing it. I gathered that I was supposed to study the habits of the squirrels to ascertain where to put the trap. But I already knew their habits. The squirrels went up and the broken shells came down. And I already knew where to place the trap—at the base of the tree where they'd built their nest. *Toute simple, n'est-ce pas?*

So I fiddled with the trap for another hour or so, trapping my arm a few times before I got the knack of coordinating the little lever attached to the bait pan with the little lever attached to the collapsible ends. Then I baited it with a few peanuts, carried it outside, and set it in the grass at the base of the oak tree. But as I did so, the peanuts rolled off the bait pan. And when reaching inside to replace them, I collapsed the trap on my arm again.

" . . . sunnuvabitch trap!"

"Sacre bleu!" Elaine called from the bedroom window. "Est-ce que tu veux du Gatorade?"

"Not yet," I told her. "But could you bring me some peanut butter?"

Elaine obliged. I stuck my finger in the jar of Smuckers Natural Creamy, spread the peanut butter on the bait pan, and pressed the peanuts into the peanut butter, which held them fast. Then I set the trap again and waited until dark to place it at the base of the oak tree, so Owen and Adrian wouldn't mess with it after school.

Next morning, as soon as the school bus left, I went out back to check the trap. But instead of a panicky *écureuil gris* scurrying back and forth, an enormous *gris opossum* was wedged in the trap, so big and fat that it was now shaped like a trapezoid—just like the fallen leaves in the tumbrel had assumed the shape of a casket.

Elaine howled when I told her, but it wasn't funny. That opossum was snarling and hissing, baring the sharp teeth in its snout. Putting on my heavy leather work gloves, I gingerly grabbed the wire handle, put the cage in the trunk of the Nova, and drove out into the country beyond the university, where I set the trap down, opened the collapsible ends, and scurried into the car while the opossum exited. Which it did after a while, when it finally realized it was free to go. Ambling into the roadside ditch like a four-legged trapezoid.

. . .

Before long I got the knack of that trap and began to catch a few gray squirrels, large and small. But within a day or two, of course, they returned to our backyard from their little excursions into the country, coming right back as if they knew the way—either the very same squirrels or their local relatives—costing us a small fortune in peanuts and Smuckers Natural Creamy.

"C'est la guerre!" I told Elaine. But I knew in my heart that this particular yard war could never be won. The only way to get rid of those squirrels—and the neighborhood pigeons as well—was to move, as we would do at the end of that summer. Which proved to be a Xerox copy of the previous summer. With a few new twists.

It all began on the very day that school let out, the first day of summer vacation, when Owen and Adrian got off the school bus.

"I'm calling the police," Owen announced, "to arrest Mr. Riess."

"Nils?" Elaine said.

The school had been engaged in a nonsmoking campaign aimed at the elementary kids—800 students in grades K–12 were housed in the same building—with the goal of nipping any bad habits in the bud before the long idle days of summer. As part of the campaign, students had been encouraged to make posters, write essays, and report kids who smoked, so peer pressure could work its wiles.

Earlier that year—again for the protection of the elementary kids—the school had joined the statewide campaign about seatbelts: *Buckle Up, Ohio!* Unfortunately, Owen had been with me when I pulled into the drive-up window at the bank, removing my seatbelt to access my wallet. Whereupon a policeman, conveniently stationed beside the window, had issued me a warning. I wanted to plead entrapment, but I didn't want to create a scene (*goddam sunnuvabitch cop!*). After which Owen—recognizing my frailty—became the family's self-appointed seatbelt enforcer.

Owen always listened carefully to his teachers and got excited about these programs. And became the self-appointed enforcer of their lessons on adults.

"Did you call the police yet?" I asked.

"I just got home," Owen said. "Give a kid a break!"

As he headed for the phone book I caught him by the ear. "Let me handle this," I said. "I'll talk to Mr. Riess myself. Neighbor to neighbor, man to man. You just make sure that Adrian keeps away from cigarettes."

"No way," Adrian piped up. "Cigarettes are stinky!"

Ironically, Nils and other smokers at the university were in for a surprise that fall when the administration declared the campus a smoke-free environment, forcing faculty members, secretaries, and students to huddle furtively outside for their nicotine fix—in all kinds of weather—beneath a distinctly purple haze. Owen was delighted to hear it.

Then there was Bernie Lawson, a sad only child who lived next door, his yard abutting our side yard to the north. He was the same age and in the same grade as Owen. His father was rarely around and his mother hid in the house all day—I never once talked to her during our year and a half on Christopher Circle—leaving Bernie to his own devices. Without the experience of siblings, Bernie never learned how to relate to the flock of neighborhood pigeons, which flew back and forth with siblings galore. This made him a pariah, the neighborhood black sheep, until he latched onto Owen as his "best friend." And refused to unlatch. Morning, noon, and night Bernie Lawson was at our door asking for Owen or swinging on the swing set or climbing into the play-fort.

Alone.

One day that summer I found Bernie in our backyard, rapping on the screen door to our screened-in and roofed-over deck. "Is Owen home?" he asked. His voice was weak and pathetic, and I felt sorry for him.

"I thought he was," I said. But Owen and Adrian were nowhere to be seen. And the neighborhood was strangely quiet.

Several hours later, when Owen and Adrian returned, Elaine asked them where they'd been. They were all excited. Their mouths were full of penny candy and their fists held something that looked like baseball cards.

"Backyard Bible School!" Owen said. "Everyone was there! At the Allens'!"

"Look what we won!" Adrian said. He opened his fist, displaying some sort of religious bookmark with a beatific image of Jesus Rising.

"How'd you win that stuff?" I asked.

"We had to memorize some verses from the Bible," Owen said. "But I forgot them already!"

"Sacre bleu!" Elaine said under her breath.

The alternative to Backyard Bible School was Bernie Lawson. Things were closing in on us from all sides. There was nothing to do but call the realtor.

Yard Wars of the Ohio Outback

County Road 50

We lived for the next year and a half in Lima (pronounced like the bean), not far from Furrows, my favorite store for yard war ammunition.

Unfortunately, now that we lived so close to this ally, I had no yard to tend. Which drove me nuts. We were renting a two-bedroom townhouse, fourth from the right in a row of eight, with a tree lawn beyond the sidewalk and a few shrubs beneath the front windows. But a community maintenance man mowed the grass and trimmed the bushes. I had nothing to do except to care for the cars out front—washing the Nova and Merry Monza every weekend and keeping them free of ice and snow in winter.

The backyard consisted of a small cement patio flanked by two lengths of alternate-board fencing that stood perpendicular to the house. No fencing joined those two sections across the rear. There was nothing but a small brook back there anyway—a scruffy gulch, really, in front of a wooded swamp—and the patio stood open to this natural view. Such as it was.

In the spring, of course, that waterway flooded, much to the delight of Owen and Adrian, covering the patio and coming within inches of entering the townhouse through the sliding glass door to the living room. But that was not my war to fight. Still, when the waters receded, I had to hose the patio clean of mud and worms.

The only other yard war during our time in Lima upset me more than that flood. It occurred during our second winter there, just before we moved to County Road 50, and it centered on the large green metal box that sat at the end of the row between the sidewalk and the curb. A large green box responsible for electricity to all units.

Snow had been falling since noon, and area schools had let their charges out early. We'd kept Owen and Adrian in school in Ada—so as not to disorient them any more than Christopher Circle already had—and they commuted with me the twenty miles or so daily. Elaine was at work at the Lima Library, where she'd taken a part-time job. It was Friday afternoon, the weekend was upon us, the snow was falling, and I was anticipating a pay-per-view boxing match on television that night, a championship bout that was costing me $29.95, a pretty penny in those days.

This was in the era of Mike Tyson, the teenage thug who was slugging his way to the heavyweight championship of the world. I'd grown up watching the Friday night fights on television with my father and grandfather, long before the days of cable TV and pay-per-view, and I had an extra stake in this particular evening of boxing—I was in training to moonlight as a licensed professional boxing judge in the state of Ohio.

The most popular charity event at the university was an annual amateur boxing night, for which I volunteered to serve as one of the judges. Now I was eager to move into the professional ranks, practicing my skills on what I hoped would be a close title fight, one that would go the distance, turning off the sound so as not to be distracted by the crowd noise and observations of the commentators. The preliminary bouts would provide me with more practice. They were to begin at 8:00 P.M., with the main event to follow at 11:00, by which time Owen and Adrian would be sound asleep.

The snow continued during dinner, burying the Nova and Merry Monza and adding to the excitement I was already feeling about the upcoming fights. But at 6:00 P.M., just as we were having dessert, the power went off throughout the neighborhood. Since it was winter, the day was already dark, and Owen and Adrian were afraid. We had no candles, no flashlights, no source of light and heat beyond a book of matches.

Instinctively, I put on my boots, ski jacket, and ski cap and went out to check the large green electrical box at the end of the row. Sitting on top of it was a small red car. Its driver, a local teenager, had been doing donuts in the parking lot in the deep snow—his tracks were plainly visible in his headlights, which were still shining—enjoying himself immensely until he'd spun out of control and knocked out the box.

. . . sunnuvabitch nincompoop!

I was livid. I was going to miss my pay-per-view match because of this kid's stupid joyriding. Heavy snow was now burying my career as a boxing judge—along with my $29.95—beneath that red car and green box.

At 6:30 a truck from the power company arrived on the scene. The police had already rocked the teenager's red car from the large green box, issued him a ticket, and towed his car away. There was nothing to do but wait.

At 7:30 the lights blinked on in all the windows along the street, then blinked off again just as suddenly. Apparently the red car had damaged an important conduit. A new part was needed. Again, there was nothing to do but wait. So I stood out there in the cold, watching and waiting, while Elaine tended to Owen and Adrian inside.

Under different circumstances, it would have been a lovely evening—the snow lay soft and deep, the power company men were loud and spirited, and someone showed up with coffee as hot and steaming as I was. The preliminary bouts were already under way, but I hoped the power would be restored for the main event.

At 8:30 the new part arrived, by 9:00 it was installed and the lights blinked on in all the windows in the row. Then blinked off again just as suddenly. The new part—not quite the right size—had blown the fixture into which it'd been inserted. So the power company men radioed for another part, which arrived at 10:30, and by 11:00, as windows were lighting up again along the length of the street, I rushed inside, grabbed my score sheet, and turned on the TV. The bell had just sounded—Round 1 was seconds old—when the champ swung a wild right and KO'd the challenger.

Which is exactly what I wanted to do to that teenager.

. . .

We moved again on the first of April—April Fools' Day—hoping the joke wouldn't be on us. But the irony of that day wouldn't be evident for years to come.

Our new home, a ranch with dark-green panel siding and a light brick front, was in the form of a T tilted ninety degrees to the left. The garage sat at the bottom of the crossbar, the boys' bedrooms were at the top, and the master bedroom was at the far end of the long stem. All right in the middle of an open country acre—43,560 square feet of peace and quiet.

That acre was exactly one mile from Christopher Circle, which intersected the road that paralleled the university campus. Within our little college town this road was known as Lima Avenue, but when it extended straight out into the farmland beyond the corporation limits to the west, its named changed to County Road 50. And that one long country mile made all the difference, putting us beyond the campus into the corn and soybeans. Only half a dozen homes were strung out along the way, on plots of one-acre minimum, guaranteeing the kind of solitude and privacy we'd enjoyed in southwest Virginia.

The ironic event that occurred that day involved the power company again—a different power company from the one that had serviced our blackout in Lima—and a squirrel. Not the *écureuil gris* kind from Christopher Circle but the fat, red bushy-tailed-gnaw-through-your-powerline type. Owen and Adrian were in school, so they were spared what followed, which would have sent them running to the SPCA.

The moving van had just arrived and the driver was having trouble backing into our gravel driveway, because the road was flanked by V-shaped ditches on both sides—ditches joined beneath the surface at the mouth of the driveway by a corrugated metal pipe. Ditches like these, which line the roads throughout northwest Ohio, are made necessary by the flatness of the land. Not far from the university, on a highway parallel to County Road 50, is an embossed historical marker dedicated to the engineer who, in the nineteenth century, determined the proper pitch of the ditch—the precise gentle slope necessary to get the water moving—enabling pioneers to drain the vast majority of the Great Black Swamp for farming.

Averaging five feet in depth, these V-shaped roadside ditches funnel water into canal-like runs, which channel it further to local creeks and streams that connect to rivers such as the Ottawa and Maumee. Which in turn flow north, all the way to Lake Erie.

But the moving van couldn't even make it into our driveway. The driver kept cutting back and forth between the ditches on both sides of the street.

Our new gravel driveway was the mirror image of a capital P, the long stem of which led directly to the garage, with space to the left for turning and parking. But the previous owner had lined that driveway with old telephone poles—where she got them, she didn't say—providing further obstacles to the van. Our acre was contoured like a contact lens, with the house in the pupil of the eyeball. But, having grown up in the flat terrain of northwest Ohio, the previous owner believed that her driveway was so steep that her car would roll away—into the ditches or right out into County Road 50—so she'd lined the perimeter of the driveway with unsightly telephone poles.

Totally frustrated, the van driver finally pulled into the long gravel driveway opposite ours, which led to a ramshackled cottagelike farmhouse sitting at the front of eight acres, and, after a good deal of angling and jockeying, successfully backed up to our garage, a feat made more difficult by an enormous oak across the road—one of the oldest, tallest, and fattest in all of Hardin County—the branches of which hung over our neighbor's ditch, County Road 50, and our ditch as well.

During these moving van maneuvers, a fat red squirrel was perched atop the telephone pole across from the front corner of our lot, gnawing on the live black wire—the very wire that crossed to a similar pole in our backyard to supply our power. We didn't notice it, of course, until it had chewed through the insulation, igniting itself and the top of that pole like the Olympic flame. Killing our power in the process.

I'd just let myself into the house to open the garage door from within, when suddenly the automatic opener wouldn't work. So I pulled the release lever, opened the door manually, and stepped outside. Where Elaine and the movers were staring in wonder at the Olympic torch of County Road 50.

"Let's ask the neighbors if we can use their phone," Elaine suggested finally. So we crossed the street to the little cottage while the movers began carting our stuff inside.

Our new neighbors, Bob and Falita Allen—no relation to the Allens who ran the Backyard Bible School on Christopher Circle—were a congenial couple in their eighties. Falita put on a pot of tea while we called the power company and watched the flaming squirrel through their front window.

Half an hour later a utility truck pulled up out front with one of those platform ladders on top. The telephone pole was still blazing, sending up a long thin stream of black smoke. A burly lineman jumped out from behind the wheel, surveyed the situation, and filled his hardhat with water from the Allens' ditch. It had been a rainy spring to date, and the ditches were still carrying about three inches of water. Then, guiding himself aloft on the cherry-picker platform, the lineman ceremoniously doused the Olympic flame, leaving the squirrel's charred carcass upright in rigor mortis. A slight tap was all it took to knock that roasted rodent into the ditch like the statue of a toppled dictator.

Then the power was restored, and we moved on in, never suspecting that the immolation of that red squirrel was a warning—a declaration of a seven-year battle that would culminate in a brutal face-to-face, tooth-and-claw encounter.

. . .

But that lengthy yard war wouldn't begin until long after my very first struggle on County Road 50. With those ugly telephone poles lining the driveway.

Eighteen feet wide at the mouth, our gravel driveway measured seventy-five feet from the house to the edge of the road. With the extra parking area to the left, it totaled 2,500 square feet. Every inch of which—with the exception of the entrance, of course—was lined with telephone poles, a dozen or more, fifteen to twenty feet long. Not only were these unsightly, they lay on the edge of the grass, which had to be trimmed by hand because the Lawn Boy could only get so close. Even when I rubbed the wheel of the Lawn Boy right up against those suckers, the stubborn grass grew thick beneath their rounded contours.

"Why don't you cut 'em up for firewood?" Elaine suggested, since our new ranch home came with a fireplace in the family room. It was a good idea. But the telephone poles were hard as rock, so old and soaked with creosote that I couldn't get my electric chain saw through them, let alone my bow saws, although it was evident that at some point they'd been cut into thirds.

"Sell them?" Elaine said. Another good idea. So I placed an ad in the local paper: "Landscaping timbers. $1.00 per foot." Which generated exactly one response.

"I'll be right over," the caller said. But he never came.

A few weeks later I ran another ad: "Landscaping timbers. Yours for the taking." Which generated no response whatsoever. There was nothing to do but roll those suckers into the back yard and leave them on our rear property line, along the edge of the cornfield. Hundreds of acres of farmland stretched away behind us—newly plowed and planted in spring corn—with a fifty-acre woodlot on the distant horizon. An idyllic scene soon to be underscored with telephone poles.

I slid my iron pike beneath a pole at the mouth of the driveway and lifted it up to get the pole rolling, then kicked it along with the heel of my foot, guiding it with my pike like Paul Bunyan. The chore took an entire Saturday morning, at the end of which our rear border was lined with "landscaping timbers," unseen from County Road 50 due to the contact lens contour of the yard.

But the problem of grass around those telephone poles remained. It still had to be trimmed by hand. And if I didn't trim it—as we soon found out—it grew knee-high, a haven for rabbits and field mice.

The next idea was my own. "I'll bury them!" I told Elaine.

"You're crazy," she said.

"Just wait and see!"

"I'll get some Gatorade when I go shopping," she said.

So off she went shopping with Owen and Adrian while I marched off with my mattock, shovel and pike to dig a three-foot deep trench across the entire length of our new backyard. Which took the rest of the weekend.

Unlike the soil in southwest Virginia, our Ohio soil was gray, not red—the result of its high clay content. Neat piles of this gray earth soon lined the grass along the edge of my trench, to be filled back in after I'd rolled the telephone poles into their mass grave, spreading the excess between the rows of newly planted corn just beyond.

But it didn't take long for those telephone poles to come back to haunt me. As I said, it'd been a rainy spring, and the next good rain returned those waterproof poles to the surface, bobbing like Lincoln Logs in a muddy bathtub. I should have known better.

Goddam . . . creosote!

Most farms in northwest Ohio contain ponds for livestock, because there's plenty of water beneath the surface and plenty of clay to hold it in place. Excavated into bowl-shaped depressions with a bulldozer, these ponds are lined with riprap, chunky gravel ten sizes larger than the grade used for driveways. Most homes in the country have ponds as well, for fishing and swimming. But we didn't need a pond—our new home came with an above-ground swimming pool, much to the delight of Owen and Adrian. And that was just as well. Having just dug a long bathtub for telephone poles, I was not about to widen it for lap swimming. Instead, I wedged those poles out with my pike and was back to square one.

What now?

My first thought was to dig a deeper bathtub. Which I tried, only to strike water in the first six inches, forcing me to bail like mad and fill the trench back in. Meanwhile, Owen and Adrian wanted me to forget the telephone poles and remove the cover from the pool. I knew nothing about pools, except that the cover on ours was depressed in the middle by a large puddle of wet leaves. But I was in the middle of a telephone pole war and refused to surrender.

As luck would have it, Eleanor Green, my department chair at the university, provided a solution. She owned an old house on Main Street in the center of Ada, with a narrow street on one side and a brick alley across the rear. Townspeople as well as students often parked along that curbless side street, and over time this had not only killed the grass there but widened and lengthened the dirt spot that replaced it. Which, depending on the weather, alternated between a mud hole or a dustbowl. Given the rainy spring, it was currently a mud hole.

"I'm thinking of getting some big rocks," Eleanor said, "to line the edge of the yard and keep the cars out." We were at her annual spring picnic for the faculty, and Eleanor, in a chef's hat and apron, was grilling hotdogs. We'd all had a few beers.

"Would you like some landscaping timbers?" I said. "I'm running a special. They're free. And I'll deliver them myself!"

Eleanor accepted, so I had to make good on my promise. Once I'd sobered up.

A few days later I rolled those telephone poles back out front to their original position along our gravel driveway. Then I drove to Furrows and purchased a heavy chain with a large hook on each end, plus a dozen eight-inch screws with a circular eye on the head, a much larger version of the kind used in latching screen doors. These I screwed into the end of each telephone pole until only the circular eye protruded. It was hard work, and the smell of creosote gave me a whanging headache.

"Gatorade?" Elaine called from the house.

"And two aspirins, please," I called back.

Then, hooking the chain to the rear of the Nova, I headed down County Road 50 in first gear, a telephone pole in tow, leaving a dark line of creosote down the middle of the pavement as if the telephone pole was a giant Magic Marker. When I passed Christopher Circle, the neighbors stood on the corner and shook their heads. I could tell they were happy we'd moved.

Then I made a wide left turn onto Main Street and a wide right turn a few blocks later, depositing those poles, one by one, along the length of Eleanor's side yard. She was thrilled, of course, but I had to caution her in case of floods: "The creosote will make them float!"

Ditch Watch

Hardin County Road 50 begins in rural farmland two and a half miles east of the village of Ada and runs due west to the county line six miles away. The middle mile of this straight stretch, a residential section bisected by State Route 235 (Main Street in Ada), is known as Lima Avenue and falls under the jurisdiction of the village. Here the speed limit drops to thirty-five miles per hour, but on County Road 50, to the east and west, there are no signs, and the local traffic is fast.

East of Ada, County Road 50 is oppressively flat, but to the west—where I live—it rolls a bit, cresting and dipping three times before it reaches the county line, so that oncoming cars are momentarily hidden. The surrounding farmland, interrupted by occasional woodlots, is seasonally devoted to corn, soybeans, and winter wheat. On the whole, the countryside appears much the way it did to those who settled the area a century and a half ago.

Grassy drainage ditches accompany County Road 50 the entire length of its run. They measure ten feet wide from the edge of the road and range in depth from a few inches to as much as seven feet. At their shallowest they have the contour of a check mark; at their deepest they are more nearly V-shaped. Channeled at intervals beneath the road, these ditches join larger waterways that run north to Hog "Crick" and Grass Run outside of Ada then west to the Ottawa River, which continues north to the Maumee. In theory, and with a lot of luck, a toy boat placed in the ditch along the road could make it all the way to Lake Erie. Or you could skate there after a deep freeze.

If a man's home is his castle, then his ditch is his moat, especially after a heavy rain. Not that we need to defend our privacy out here in the country. There are only fourteen homes strung out along the road's final two miles, set back from the ditches on plots of one to five acres with nothing but farmland for a backyard. Most were built since the sixties, although a few go back to the turn of the century. Two have been replaced after burning to the ground, at a time when water in the ditch might have helped the volunteer firemen.

But on the day we moved in, our ditch was an enemy. It was thirty-five degrees and drizzling, the water running ankle deep through a galvanized pipe beneath our driveway. The neck of the drive is only eighteen feet wide—the same width as the paved surface of County Road 50—and the movers spent half an hour backing the van in, trying to avoid the ditch to either side as well as the parallel ditch on the north side of the road. The ruts they left in the lawn are still visible, an ugly reminder of the wet spring of 1989.

That night the temperature dipped below freezing, and at dawn a car slid into the ditch just to the east of us, clipping off a utility pole at its base. On each of the next two mornings there were crumpled cars off the road at the same spot, and I realized that these country ditches were to be reckoned with.

A friend from Wood County tells me that folks out his way routinely burn their ditches, to stunt the scrub brush and facilitate drainage—everybody standing along the roadside leaning on rakes, the ditches ablaze and smoking for miles. At the university I met a student whose uncle, David Aller, is one of the few people certified to burn ditches in Hancock County. He does it as a sideline, and apparently it's quite an art. Most of his work is at intersections and near corners where the wild growth obscures the traffic. But I've never seen the ditches afire along County Road 50. The farmers, homeowners, and Hardin County personnel keep them relatively free of vegetation, although thorny locust trees tend to establish themselves readily, escaping from neighboring hedgerows and windbreaks.

Hardin County assistant engineer Mike Smith says that the road is resurfaced with a two-inch cold mix every ten years or so and receives a chip-and-seal treatment on a two-year cycle after that. The ditches, however, get more attention. Seven times a year—May 10 through the end of October—county employee Bob Leis cuts the grass along a right-of-way between the edge of the road and the telephone poles. He uses a John Deere diesel tractor with a ten-foot cutting arm and a five-foot-wide flail behind. The tractor's two front tires are about the size of those of a pickup truck, but the two rear tubeless tires stand five feet tall. Keeping the left wheel on the berm and the right wheel in the grass of the ditch, Leis makes sure that his first cut is not too severe. It's on his second pass that the debris turns up. Then the flail goes to work—a heavy roller containing thirty-six knife blades covered by a metal shell—pulverizing the bottles, beer cans, and other trash. Leis gets fewer flat tires from broken glass these days—about three a summer—because the front tractor tires now contain a foam that seals off punctures.

Since the grass is thick and tough in the spring, Leis can make only one pass with the tractor on his first time out. A few years ago, in an effort to protect the pheasants and other birds that nest in the ditches, the state of Ohio required all mowers to make but a single pass until mid-July, when the birds come up and take cover among the crops in the field. The strategy seems to be working. Leis saw more pheasants this past summer than in previous years. I've seen them, too—a bonus of my daily ditch watch—on afternoon jogs to the county line and back, and Bob Leis was glad to hear it.

Often, while mowing, Leis has to raise the cutting bar on his tractor to avoid hitting snakes, baby raccoons, and other living creatures in the ditch. Cats are the biggest problem—they wait until the last second to move away. He's afraid he'll cut off their legs. Dogs are a problem too. Running out from the neighboring yards to bark at the tractor, they put themselves in danger of the traffic, so Leis has to stop work and get their owners after them. He also sees a lot of dead dogs and cats. "People just throw 'em in the ditch," he says, "to get rid of them."

Once, Leis hit a skunk and went stinking for a week. On another occasion, when the rear wheels of his tractor crunched a six-pack, he got squirted with beer and returned to the garage smelling like a drunk. But sometimes he gets lucky, as when five dollars came rolling up out of the ditch one day, sticking to the tractor wheel—the only money he's found in ten years on the job. The biggest danger he faces is turning over, because the ditch occasionally drops off sharply, leaving the tractor riding at steep angles. But his greatest fear is people. He's afraid of getting slammed by drunks on the road. Yet most people, he concedes, are pretty courteous. When it's foggy, he simply doesn't mow. Occasionally, the farmers will get after him about cutting too close to their crops, but in general the complaints are few. All in all, to hear Bob Leis tell it, there are worse jobs than mowing the ditches in Hardin County.

For those of us who live along County Road 50 and subscribe to the *Lima News*, the ditches out front pose a challenge of a different sort. Not so if you take the *Kenton Times*, because the *Times* supplies its customers with a blue-and-white monogrammed box that can be attached to the post of your mailbox. But the *Lima News* is flung from the window of a passing vehicle that barely slows to fifty miles an hour. The paper is rolled and secured with an elastic band that often breaks on impact, scattering the paper along the ditch. In wet weather it comes in a thin blue-plastic wrapper, but even that can get chewed up enough as it hits the gravel driveway so that the paper explodes and blows away. Or, if it lands in the ditch—either short of the driveway or beyond it—water seeps in through the open end of the wrapper, making the paper unreadable. Often I've had to purchase another at the Dairy Mart in Ada because ours got destroyed in delivery. But if the paper were put in our mailbox, it would take the carrier twice as long to do the route and cost twice as much in gasoline, what with all the stopping and starting. Such is the price—to customer and carrier—of country living with a ditch by the side of the road.

Not long after hunting for the *Lima News* became part of my daily ditch watch, something happened to put that problem in perspective. One Saturday night in May of 1989, an Ada man and a Lafayette woman heading west on County Road 50 plowed through the ditch about a mile to the west of us and struck a tree at the edge of the woodlot there. Neither was wearing a seatbelt, and the man was killed. The woman, who was driving, explained that the car had gone off the edge of the road to the right, then swerved back across the road into the woods. The ditches at that point fall away immediately to a depth of three feet, so disaster was waiting on either side. Had the car continued to the right, it would have rolled several times into the fields. A year later, on the anniversary of the accident, a white wooden cross and a spray of plastic flowers were placed in the ditch at the base of the fatal tree. In the interval I noticed mute evidence of other mishaps that might have proved just as tragic—black skid marks veering toward the ditches in summer and muddy ruts through the ditches in winter, all coming to an abrupt and chilling halt.

It's a wonder more people haven't been killed, especially where County Road 50 reaches County Road 15, County Line Road. County Road 50 should come to an end there, forcing motorists to stop and turn north or south. But the road slants sharply to the left for ten yards or so, creating a wide and dangerous intersection, before heading due west again toward Lima as Lafayette Road. Cars coming east at that point often end up in the fields on the south side of the road, unable to negotiate the quick turn. Last January, after a stretch of foggy weather produced numerous tire tracks in the fields, three small metal reflectors were installed on stakes at the end of County Road 50 to catch the headlights of motorists coming out of Allen County. In February I found the first of those stakes flat against the earth and straddled by muddy tire tracks, a wheel cover lying nearby. In March the other two were leveled. In the fall of 1992 yellow lines were painted down the center of the road, but drivers tend to ignore them. By defining lanes, the lines seem to narrow the distance to the ditches.

Dale Badertscher, who farms 220 acres along County Road 50, has pulled his share of vehicles out of the ditches and fields over the years. At one point, when the land he rents was fenced in for cattle, eastbound cars used to miss that sharp turn at least once a month. He was always chasing cattle and repairing the fence. Last winter I asked him about a set of deep tracks that ran through the ditch into the field to the north of the road, missing a utility pole by three feet. He said that a neighbor had heard the car, and the driver was "going faster than he should have." Which is usually the case.

Badertscher has been farming the land along County Road 50 for the last eighteen years, and for seven years before that with his father. He's got a collection of more than a hundred arrowheads that he's found in the fields as he works. And counted among his souvenirs is a green Coke bottle that turned up one day when his plow caught a piece of the ditch. "When's the last time you saw a Coke bottle like that?" he asks. Like Bob Leis, he gets a few flat tires each season from glass bottles in the field. In the old days bottles and cans would hurt the combine, but the newer equipment, he says, just "chops 'em up and spits 'em back." Any debris that gets into the grain is cleaned in the processing. And, like Leis, he has found a few dollar bills on the job. Yet his most precious find has proved priceless—a puppy, part Husky, that was abandoned in the ditch just after weaning. The dog, named Tippy for its white-tipped tail, has been a part of the Badertscher family for eleven years now.

During the course of last winter, I noticed many tracks through the ditches on my daily jog to the county line and back. They always seem to be made after dark, and they all occur in the final mile of County Road 50, where there are only two houses—a new ranch owned by Richard Klingler on the north side of the road and an old empty farmhouse just opposite, in front of the big red barn and outbuildings that are very much in use and bear the name of Warren and Zelma Lacey. These buildings lie just to the west of the intersection with St. Paul Road (Liberty Township 15), and from there, once you pass the woodlot that claimed the life of the Ada man, it's an open roller-coaster ride to the county line.

The scariest tracks, left by two vehicles, appeared in front of the Klingler place after a snowstorm, one set tearing up his lawn and the other knocking out the chain-link fence in front of the empty farmhouse across the street—as if approaching cars had swerved through the ditches to avoid a head-on collision. A few days later, after the February ice storm that caused so many accidents throughout the state, I traced a curious and continuous set of tracks through the field just to the east of Richard Klingler's home. A vehicle, heading west, had cut through the ditch at the intersection of St. Paul Road, running parallel to County Road 50 for several hundred yards, then cut back through the ditch to the road again. The storm had caused a whiteout, and perhaps the driver had lost his way. Or maybe the maneuver had been done on purpose, since drifting snow was closing the roads. I would have felt more comfortable about those tracks in the field had the driver not emerged from the ditch so close to a utility pole.

Bob Allen Jr., who grew up in the farmhouse across the street from us, has a whiteout story with a happier ending. It was 1935, and Allen, later mayor of Ada, was in the first grade. School was let out early—about 2:00 P.M.—because of a winter storm. The temperature was thirty below, the snow was blowing and drifting, and the visibility was zero. The school bus came to a halt on St. Paul Road and could go no farther, so Allen and a dozen other children were let off to walk home. The first boy out the door stepped into the ditch and sank waist-high in snow. Then the bigger kids carried the smaller kids across the fields, where the snow wasn't as deep, to Paul Klingler's place. But the Klinglers had no phone. Back on County Road 50, Allen's parents were beginning to worry. His mother, Falita, who passed away last year, was pregnant at the time and had a broken leg as well. When darkness fell, his father set out west to Isaiah Klingler's, the only home in the area with a telephone. It was only a quarter of a mile away, but he almost didn't make it, falling down several times, hunched over into the teeth of the wind, making his way along a fence at the back of the ditch. At Isaiah's place he learned that the kids were all safe at Paul's, but it was 9:00 P.M. before he could get back to tell his wife. The children, enjoying the holiday, returned home the next day on horse-drawn sleds.

The Allen home sits across the street from us on several acres of land that are screened from view by a row of junipers along the back of the ditch. The bushes, ten feet tall and six feet deep, run for seventy-five yards from the east corner of the property to the gravel driveway in the middle of the lot. Beyond the driveway, however, they continue only another six yards. I once asked Falita Allen what happened to the rest of the row.

Well, she said, one afternoon a few years ago they heard a strange noise out front. A car heading toward Ada had gone off the road, cut across the ditch, and mowed down the junipers, ending up on top of the bushes, wheels spinning. The driver, a young man in his early twenties, climbed down and wandered into the house to use the telephone, but Robert Allen Sr. asked him to leave, since the man was obviously drunk or on drugs. The car had to be pulled off the junipers with a backhoe. Meanwhile, the driver disappeared. Later that evening Fred Lissner, who lives to the west of the Allen property beyond a large field, saw a light on in his car outside. The door was open. Someone had been fooling with the car. Then his neighbor across the street reported a car missing. The keys had been in it. Police traced the license of the car on the junipers and found the young man who had stolen the neighbor's car. The Allens replaced the bushes with some other small shrubs, but the huge gap in the row is still very much evident.

A more stately landmark on the Allen property stands among the junipers just to the east of the driveway: one of the largest oak trees in Hardin County. The tree is so huge that if you stand right up against the trunk and spread your arms wide, anyone standing beyond the tree can't see your fingertips. The branches—thick and gnarled— overhang the ditches on both sides of the road. Bob Allen says that that tree was enormous when he was a kid, and when people like the Klinglers were settling the area in the 1800s they used to have picnics in the shade of its branches. "When you live in a place," he reminisced, "you don't realize it's a part of history."

Many members of the Klingler family are buried in the country graveyard on St. Paul Road, where the tombstones date to the Civil War. And some of the marble slabs there—especially those that face west—go back even farther, the inscriptions rubbed smooth by the wind and rain. Anna Belle Klingler, who is in her seventies, is the mother of Richard Klingler and the widow of Keith Klingler, who went to school with Falita and Robert Allen Sr. She's been in the area for sixty years and has lived on County Road 50—where Isaiah Klingler used to live—since 1953, in the last home to the west of us before St. Paul Road. She can recall when there was only one house between herself and Ada. The house she lives in was built in the forties to replace the one that burned down, "a big old sixteen-room farmhouse that had runnin' water and a bathroom when no one else did." The furnace just exploded one October—stovepipe combustion due to an accumulation of dust in the registers—when her mother-in-law went to start it up for the winter. "And that," Anna Belle laughs, "was the first and last fire of the year."

Anna Belle, whose mother was Mary Belle, owns the land that Dale Badertscher farms. She says that all the neighborhood farmers worked together to get a waterway put in, laying drainage tiles in their fields to get the water to the roadside ditches and beyond. Her son Richard owns the Lacey farm across from his ranch house down the road, but he's not a farmer. He works for a Japanese firm in Bluffton because, as Anna Belle says, "You can't get rich on a farm."

Between Main Street in Ada and County Line Road, County Road 50 is intersected only twice—by St. Paul Road to the west of us and Liberty Township 35, known as Klingler Road, to the east, each one mile apart. According to Anna Belle, the Klinglers came to America from Germany in the early nineteenth century, but it's impossible to keep them all straight. A family tree made in 1910 dates back to an Amos Klingler, who had six or seven sons and one daughter, and, before that, to Amos's father, who had eighteen children. The original family tree has been lost, but Sam Klingler had copies made up for a family reunion a few years ago. He was 100 years old at the time.

"Now you take the Lacey farm," Anna Belle says. "Warren and Zelma were brother and sister. His grandma and my husband's father were first cousins. Warren was married once, but his wife run him off with a butcher knife. When he passed away he left the place to Zelma, who died an old maid a few years ago, at the age of ninety-seven."

Fred Lissner, who lives across from Anna Belle, jogs daily along County Road 50, like me, except that he's been doing it longer—for more than thirteen years now—and he goes farther, a mile or two into Allen County on Lafayette Road, before turning back. He says he used to see an old lady sitting on the porch at the Lacey place— that would have been Zelma—and he'd wave and cross to the far side of the road so as not to frighten her. The Lissners live in a ranch house built to replace their Victorian-style clapboard farmhouse that burned down in 1982. They had gone to Lima one Sunday afternoon and when they returned, their old house, which used to sit just thirty feet back from the ditch, was a pile of blackened rubble. The cause was never determined. For a few weeks after that they lived where we do now while the previous owner was out of town.

Fred Lissner agrees that jogging along County Road 50 can be dangerous. You have to run facing traffic. As I mentioned earlier, the paved surface is only eighteen feet wide and the ditches slope away immediately. American vehicles average six feet in width, and, if cars coming from each direction keep a three-foot berth between them, that leaves only eighteen inches along the roadside for joggers. "The old folks don't really see you," Lissner says, "so you have to get the hell out of the way." Fortunately, the local traffic is light, even in the late afternoon when I usually pass Lissner somewhere along the road. It takes me thirty minutes to get to the county line and back, and in that time I won't encounter but half a dozen vehicles. Like Lissner, however, I often step down into the ditch when I hear them coming.

Lissner has seen every kind of animal, dead and alive, along the road and in the ditches over the years—dogs, cats, groundhogs, possum, raccoons, snakes, skunks. He's even been chased by a flock of birds. "I'm not too sure they didn't want to attack me," he says. In the warmer months, the crows and turkey vultures take care of the roadkill, posting their sentinels in the trees of the woodlots and persistently pecking at the carrion, despite an occasional jogger or car. In the colder months the carcasses eventually get knocked into the ditches, or the injured animals crawl in there to die.

In some of the fields along County Road 50 cows graze right up to the fence at the back of the ditch. "They like to get up and talk to me," Lissner says. Sometimes the entire herd will begin to jog along with him. Like Bob Leis and Dale Badertscher, he has found a bit of cash along the road, but unlike me he doesn't concentrate on the ditches— he likes to listen for the whistles of the trains that run parallel to the road in the fields to the north, counting the boxcars or looking for passengers in the Amtrak, trying to beat them to the next intersection.

The only other jogger that goes as far as the county line and back is John Magee of Ada, who has been running the route since 1976. Magee remembers the day the Lissners' house burned down. He had seen Fred and his wife leaving for Lima as he jogged by, and later, as he was getting into the bathtub after his run, he heard sirens and could see smoke to the west. The house had been on fire as he passed it on his way back to Ada.

The Lissners had a determined hound dog that used to climb out of its pen—right over a fence topped with barbed wire—and chase Magee as he jogged by. But one day as it came barking across the yard, Magee heard a car approaching from behind, and the dog was struck and killed as it emerged from the roadside ditch.

Like the others who pass the ditches daily, Magee has found some money along County Road 50—three one-dollar bills, one after another, just lying there waiting to be picked up. But a surprise of a different sort awaited him one day, the kind that reflects the wanton freedom generated by an open country road. Not far from the county line on the south side of the road, there used to be a large tree in the ditch. You can still see the stump. One afternoon as Magee jogged by, two young men were sitting in the ditch in the shade of that tree smoking dope. "They asked me to join them," he says. The fields were green and the day was warm, but Magee continued on his way—beneath white clouds and a wide blue sky—on a high of his own.

Everybody I've talked with about the ditches along County Road 50 has found money there, except me. And yet I observe the ditches daily. Once, when my wife and I were biking along with our two boys, our older son slammed on his brakes and skidded to a halt at what appeared to be a twenty-dollar bill in the grass at the edge of the ditch. But it was only funny money, and we all felt cheated—victims of a practical joke in the middle of nowhere.

Then one November, quite suddenly, the ditches became a gold mine. A letter from Brown Refuse, which collects our trash, asked us to begin separating our garbage for recycling. This led me to look at the ditches in a new way. In the months since moving in, I hadn't really noticed the litter on my daily jog—the beer cans, the bottles, the paper—but all at once that was all I saw.

On a whim I looked up "litter" in the card catalog at the university library in Ada. There was only one entry: *Litter: The Ugly Enemy*, a nonfiction book for young adults by Dorothy E. Shuttlesworth. Published in 1973, it describes what citizens can do to clean up their communities and launch consciousness-raising campaigns against litter.

A good idea, I thought, to educate the young, but why weren't there more entries? I tried the *Reader's Guide to Periodical Literature* but found only "cat litter." Then, under "pollution," I hit the jackpot— acid rain, air pollution, chemical plants, medical waste, pesticides, radioactive waste, radon, space debris, trade waste, etc. Everything but beer cans and bottles. Compared to the rest of the environment, I guess, the ditches of Ohio are in pretty good shape. Old-fashioned litter has become a quaint item, yet it remains a very big problem, and because of it my ditch watch is turning a profit.

Inspired by the request from Brown Refuse, I began to pick up aluminum cans from the ditches on my daily jog to the county line and back, stomping them flat and putting them in a plastic bag or tucking them into the pocket of my windbreaker. In the first six months I collected 540 cans, which—at twenty-eight cents per pound—is worth six dollars at the Ice Plant Recycling Center in Ada. Based on those figures, I project an annual income of twelve dollars, seven dollars more than Bob Leis has found in twelve years of mowing the ditches in Hardin County.

Most of the cans are beer cans, with an occasional pop container. I don't pick up bottles—they're too heavy and dangerous. They're also not as plentiful. An inventory I took one January day revealed a total of eighty-four glass bottles—pop, beer, wine, and liquor—in the ditches between here and the county line. The number remains fairly constant, and I assume that this glass will eventually get crushed during the summer months by the flail on Bob Leis's tractor.

I used to think that littering was an unconscious act, but the evidence in the ditches proves otherwise. I often find, for example, a half dozen or more beer cans jettisoned in a cardboard twelve-pack container. Nearly every pop bottle I have seen has its cap on, the peeled labels often tucked inside. Several bags of trash that I've examined—from area fast food chains—contained, along with french fry bags and soft drink cups, a pile of cigarette butts from a dashboard ashtray.

The littering is constant. I average three cans a day, and I can't remember the last time I came home empty-handed. And the litterers, by and large, are the same people. Every week or so I collect several blue-and-beige Schaefer Light cans that have been crushed in an identical manner—end to end like an accordion—before they are thrown out. Generally, I find more cans on Saturday and Sunday than during the week. And almost all of the littering occurs—like the accidents and tire tracks—in the last open mile before the county line. The time of year makes no difference. I've picked up cans on Thanksgiving, Christmas, and Easter. People who litter do not take holidays.

Ordinance 521.08 of the Ada Health, Safety and Welfare Code governs "littering and the deposit of garbage, rubbish, junk, etc." Technically, bottles and cans are "rubbish" and littering is a misdemeanor punishable by a $100 fine. The Ohio Revised Code, which applies to both state and county jurisdictions, contains the same language, except that the court costs and fines are a little higher. Unfortunately, those laws are rarely enforced.

I asked Anne Boston, program manager at the Hardin County Office of Litter Prevention and Recycling, about littering in the ditches in Hardin County. She recalls an incident in the area near County Road 50 where a road was closed for bridge repairs. From the ditch there workers removed a refrigerator, three tires, pieces of concrete and brick, seven bags of trash, and a stack of old license plates. The plates were traced to an individual who had hired someone to dump the load. The offender paid a fine of $250 plus court costs, was placed on probation for a year, and had to perform four days of public service.

Anne Boston sent me the Hardin County litter crew records for 1988 and 1989. They indicate which county roads were cleaned and how many bags of trash were picked up. County Road 50 was not listed. This leads me to believe that our road is cleaner than most, since only roads specified by the supervisor get attention. The records detail the area covered, the date, the man-hours, the miles covered on foot, and the bags of litter per mile. If I were to pick up all the trash I see in the mile and a half between my home and the county line, I estimate it would fill less than one bag, so I can understand why the road hasn't been policed in recent years.

Most of the paper I see in the ditches either blows away or breaks apart after a rain. Much of it, besides the fast food bags, consists of plastic cigarette wrappers. Then there is the automobile junk—wheel covers, fan belts, exhaust pipes, and metal door strips. This stuff isn't littered but simply falls from passing vehicles, although empty oil containers and jugs of windshield fluid are often tossed into the ditches on purpose. It gets discouraging, despite the relative cleanliness of the road. But there is hope. Ohio House Bill 592 has set a goal for Ohioans to recycle 25 percent of all garbage in our waste stream within the next five years. That's a start, and the recycling habit—as I've found—can become infectious as well as profitable.

But my recycling effort by no means dominates my ditch watch. I enjoy talking to folks along County Road 50. And every season out here brings special moments. Wildflowers dot the ditches in summer.

In the fall the leaves from the Allens' big oak fill our ditch, and my boys dive into them. In winter, ditch water flows through the untouched snowdrifts like a black brush stroke. One spring I monitored a robin's nest in a locust thicket in the ditch between the Allens' and Lissners'. Each day, as I approached, the four chicks within would close their gaping beaks and rotate downward in unison into a feathery ball. The mother robin would wait until I had jogged on by before bringing her worm to the nest. Later, through binoculars from beyond the ditch across the street, I observed two of the four make their first flights into the cornfield beyond. Their abandoned nest is still in the thicket, a reminder that life comes and goes along the county ditches, and always has.

Yard Wars of the Ohio Outback

Birdminton

I had to tackle two chores in the yard before I could drag those telephone poles to Eleanor's—*chores*, not *wars*, which is why I've overlooked them. The first was to dismantle a rather large dog pen.

The previous owner, being a divorcée, had kept a large black dog to guard the house while she was at work, since her two sons, whose bedrooms Owen and Adrian now occupied, had grown up and moved out. The wire fence that contained this dog—fixed at intervals to metal stakes—enclosed the entire rear half of the east side of the yard, which lay to the left as you faced the house. Beginning at the front corner of the garage, this wire fence paralleled County Road 50 to our eastern property line, turned south to the cornfield, west across the back border, and north to the left rear corner of the house—1,250 square yards in which that large black dog had been free to roam, barking at cars and joggers out in the road.

The dog pen had two points of access for the previous owner's riding mower. The first was a double gate just to the left of the garage—two sections of cyclone fencing that swung outward—latched together by a stirrup-shaped thingy that flopped into place. The second point of access, where the fence joined the rear corner of the house, was a single gate. Both gates were hinged to hollow metal pipes sunk deep in concrete.

The guard dog on duty could protect the interior of the house through the side door to the garage, which was left ajar along with the door to the kitchen. Dutch doors in the kitchen and front hall kept the dog from the living room, dining room, and master bedroom. Closed doors to the twin bedrooms and bathroom off the family room kept it from those areas as well. Still, it could threaten you both inside and out if it had to.

To this day the wooden handrail along the steps from the garage into the kitchen is rough and ugly, chewed and clawed as it was by that dog—out of frustration for being left alone all day, or its inability to get at cars and joggers.

But that dog pen had to go, along with twelve little maple trees newly planted in four rows of three in the front half of the side yard. That was the other chore. Not only would it give me more room for rolling telephone poles, it would open the entire side yard for our ball field, a full seventy-five yards from roadside to cornfield.

Fortunately, those twelve trees were mere saplings, easily yanked out by hand and transplanted just as quickly along our east border— punching holes with my pike, shoving the roots in, and stomping the earth firm. These young trees were swamp maples, junk trees that grow like hell and branch out all over the place. Today that row, so hastily transplanted, stands sixty feet tall, trimmed straight up like a hedge to keep our ball field intact, although Owen and Adrian, like the previous owner's sons, have grown up and moved out.

Removing the dog pen was almost as easy as transplanting those maples. All I had to do was unhitch the wire fencing from the stakes and roll it into a large bale, like area farmers roll hay. I stored the bale and stakes in the basement in case I'd need them again (I would). Then I dismantled the gates, digging around the footings and smashing the concrete with a sledgehammer to free the metal pipes that the gates were hinged to. I transplanted those gate sections as well, to the middle of the rear property line where I made a small three-sided burning pen open to the prevailing west wind. It was handy for bonfires. We lived in Hardin County proper now, where, unlike in town, fires (and firing guns) were permitted in your own backyard.

A single eight-foot-long metal pipe remained after I'd erected the burning pen. This I sledge-hammered into the ground toward the east corner of our lot, afixing a birdhouse on top, hoping for bluebirds.

And the bluebirds would come.

But not before other birds on our country acre drove me to birdminton.

. . .

Our birdminton days began early one morning that spring with a dull *thunk!* waking me from a sound sleep.

I shook Elaine by the shoulder. "Did you hear that?"

"What?" she muttered.

"That dull *thunk* in the living room. There it goes again! It woke me up."

"You woke *me* up," Elaine said. "I didn't hear anything."

But she did, after the third *thunk.* And fourth. And fifth. And sixth. They were not rapid-fire *thunks—thunk!thunk!thunk!—*but intermittent *thunks.* With pauses in between. Just long enough to make you think they'd stopped, when—*thunk!*—they hadn't.

I got up to investigate, putting on my robe and stepping into the living room just in time to see a robin fly up to the picture window from the long hedge below it to head-butt its own reflection. The sight of me approaching the window, of course, was too much for that bird, and it retreated through the gray dawn to a large white pine in the center of our front yard. So I returned to bed.

"What was it?" Elaine muttered.

"Just a—" *thunk!* "—robin."

"I hear it now," Elaine said. "Thanks for pointing it out. Now I'll never—" *thunk!* "—get back to sleep!"

That robin, of course, was building a nest out front—in the hedge or white pine—defending its territory against itself in the process. Every time it flew toward the house, its own reflection came at it from the picture window, as if to beat it to the hedge. So there was nothing to do but head-butt the glass. *Thunk!* After which, a bit dazed, the robin would retreat to the white pine, until that interloper appeared again. I'd never witnessed this phenomenon before. It was survival of the fittest. And this was one fit bird.

For the next few weeks that robin became an alarm clock. At the *thunk* of dawn. Such was life in the country. But it began to get on my nerves. Before long I found myself waking up early—while Elaine snored blissfully, as did Owen and Adrian in their bedrooms at the far end of the house—waiting for that sound while thinking to myself, *Today—today, that bird won't—thunk!*

" . . . sunnuvabitch bird!"

To make matters worse, I had to clean the picture window with Windex each day. That robin must have been molding its muddy nest with its breast, which smacked the glass a millisecond after its head, tattooing it with what looked like muddy thumbprints. Elaine offered to do the Windexing, just to curb my anger, but she couldn't quite reach the entire window without a stepladder. So the chore fell to me.

Right after breakfast, as soon as the school bus left, I'd go out front between the hedge and the house with a bottle of Windex and roll of paper towels. The sparkling spring air was alive with birdsong, punctuated, as soon as I went back inside, with a *thunk* on the downbeat.

"Do you know how long that bird'll go on like that?" I asked the head of the Biology Department. But I knew the answer already. *The whole damn day!*

"Get yourself some black construction paper and make a silhouette of a cat," he advised. "Tape it to the inside of the window. That'll solve your problem."

But it didn't. That black spot only made the reflection sharper, so the robin head-butted it like a target on a firing range. My silhouette of a cat looked more like a snowman, anyway. So I tried the silhouette of an owl, with the same results. Then I gave that robin a ferocious red-tailed hawk, copying the silhouette from an illustration in my *Golden Guide to Field Identification of Birds of North America*. Right down to the wingspan. With the same results.

Thunk!

Meanwhile, we'd hired Jim Massillo to cut a window into the west wall of the master bedroom. This window—a crank-it-open type—gave us spring breezes throughout the house, since the prevailing wind was out of the west. To the left of the bed, the south wall of the bedroom featured a set of sliding glass doors that led to the Florida room, a long sunny room across the back of the house that had three sets of sliding glass doors offering more access than was needed to the backyard and pool. I locked the second two and we used only the first. And there was yet another sliding glass door on the east wall leading to an interior dining area off the family room.

In short, that Florida room was one long glass wall, one long reflected mural of the backyard and cornfield beyond. And I was not surprised that birds occasionally flew into it. But there was no hedge or pine tree handy in which to nest, from which to mount an assault on an imagined intruder. So the birds—mostly starlings, for some reason—struck the Florida room windows in headlong flight: *THUNK!* And that was that.

I'd find the dead birds on the ground, their little necks bent. Then I'd pick them up by the tail—thumb-and-finger—and toss them into my burning pen, which became their funeral pyre (after the school bus left), once I'd accumulated enough brush and twigs for a bonfire.

And so, because of the Florida room, on some mornings, as I lay awake listening for a *thunk* from out front, I'd be startled by a *THUNK* from out back—a double frustration that tripled when Jim Massillo finished the new window on our west bedroom wall.

Several dogwood trees flanked the west end of the house, and within a day or two a pair of cardinals was nesting there, the bright-red male and dull-red female taking turns *thunk*ing their own reflections in the new window to protect their unborn chicks. This new window just happened to be above the headboard to our queen-size bed, within four feet of my ear. So my spring mornings went something like this: (Picture window) *Thunk!* Pause. (Picture window) *Thunk!* (Bedroom window) *Thunk!* Pause. (Picture window) *Thunk!* (Bedroom window) *Thunk!* (Florida room) *THUNK!* After which I'd call it a day, grab my robe, and go out to fetch the morning paper.

. . .

During the *thunk*ing, Owen and Adrian kept bugging me to open the pool. It was May now. The weather had turned hot, and they were ready to take the plunge. But I wasn't. All I wanted was a good night's sleep.

To keep the boys happy, Elaine bought a badminton set, and I strung the net between its thin metal poles on the west side of the house, just outside our new bedroom window. This section of the yard was as large as our ball field to the east, except that it was shaded front and rear by two large swamp maples, both of which had branched out all over the place from multiple trunks.

The large swamp maple toward the front simultaneously overhung both the master bedroom and the power line that ran from the telephone pole across the road along the western edge of our property. The one to the rear, equally as big, lent more shade to the badminton court. I set up the net exactly between them, east-to-west. And dreamed all night of shuttlecocks attacking the bedroom window.

But the next morning, before the *thunk* of dawn, I awoke with a brilliant idea. As soon as Owen and Adrian left for school, I took down the badminton net and crisscrossed its metal poles within the frame of the picture window in the living room, stapling the net to the wooden frame itself wherever I could, stretching it up and down and back and forth to cover as much of the glass as possible. I didn't bother with the Windex. The window looked ugly enough as it was.

Along with the crisscrossed poles, the white plastic tape that lined the top of the net created the impression of a Confederate flag. But the window was protected! Any robin trying to head-butt its reflection would get caught like a fish.

"It looks awful," Elaine said. "What will you tell the boys?"

"That I'm opening the pool! It's a perfect solution."

"But we want to play volleyball in the pool!" Owen said after school. "We can hang the net across the water!" Adrian agreed. So I removed the badminton net from the picture window. And it was back to the drawing board to out*thunk* those birds.

Then my mind began whirring like an eggbeater, and off I went to Lima, returning an hour later with two minnow seines—large black nets with a much tighter weave than that of the badminton net. Stapled neatly to the frame of the picture window, the first net covered every square inch of glass. Lacking metal poles and a plastic border, it was invisible as well. I stretched the second seine from the gutter above our bedroom window to the dogwood trees below. An equally effective and invisible fence—ready to bounce those cardinals like a trampoline right back where they came from. And next morning, for the first time in weeks, I slept without interruption.

But my birdminton campaign was far from over. Who'd a thunk it? The peace lasted but a day or two. We'd just finished dinner. Owen and Adrian were outside playing badminton (I'd put the net back up, promising to open the pool on the weekend), and Elaine and I were watching the news on television. When I heard a dull metallic *clunk* in the chimney.

"Did you hear that?"

"Hear what?" Elaine said.

"That dull metallic *clunk*. In the chimney. There it goes again!"

"I don't hear anything except the dishwasher."

"Listen carefully," I said. And the sound came again. *Clunk.*

"I heard it that time," she said. "Thanks a lot. Now I can't focus on the news!"

Our chimney was faux brick with a sheet-metal flue. *Clunk.*

"Something's in there," I said to Elaine.

"Squirrels?" she suggested.

"I'll see." Which was stupid, of course, because I hadn't checked out the chimney since moving in. Nonetheless, parting the chain mail fireplace screen like drawn drapes, I opened the damper. And two startled starlings flew into my face.

"Goddam . . . birds!"

Elaine screamed as the starlings flew from room to room, window to window, seeking the light of day—only to clutch the curtains and fly off again. Meanwhile, to lessen their options, I flew about shutting doors. Then I ran into the basement and grabbed the metal tops from two old garbage cans that I kept for kindling wood.

Back upstairs, I chased those birds from wall to wall like a manic cymbal player, hoping to clap them between the garbage can lids. But it was too hard. All I could do was pin one against the wall, protecting my face from the other by using the second lid as a shield. Elaine's screaming, of course, brought the boys running inside, badminton racquets in hand.

"Give me your racquet!" I shouted at Owen. But he refused. He hadn't quite figured out what was happening—his mother was screaming and his father was flailing at the air with a garbage can lid while holding another lid flush against the wall.

But Adrian calmly offered me his racquet, which I slid along the wall to sandwich the pinned starling to the underside of the lid. Then raced outside to let the poor bird go.

The second starling didn't fare so well. Tired of its dive-bombing, I kept swatting at it with Adrian's badminton racquet, finally knocking it to the floor and covering it with one of the garbage can lids. Which I stomped on—just once—putting the lid on that bird once and for all. Then, thumb and finger, I picked it up by the tail and took it outside to my burning pen.

While Owen and Adrian denounced me as the cruelest dad ever.

Fast-forward to the following spring.

We were all gathered around the television watching *Jeopardy!* when the chimney went *clunk.*

"Here we go again," Elaine said.

"Don't you dare hurt those birds!" Owen said.

"No problem," I said. "We'll smoke 'em out!"

"What?" Adrian squeaked.

"Smoke rises," I explained. "I'll make a fire, open the damper at the last second, and those birds will fly up the chimney. What comes down must go up. It's a law of physics. All I need is a little kindling and today's paper."

While I prepared the fire, Owen and Adrian ran outside to make sure the birds exited the chimney safely. My reputation as a father was on the line.

"And this time," I told Elaine, "I'll keep the fireplace screen shut."

It was the perfect solution. But it was a disaster, of course. Because the moment I opened the damper and the flames and smoke shot upward, those dumb starlings came down, in defiance of the law of physics, their nest aflame at the very bottom of the flue.

As the smoke began rising from the chimney outside, Owen and Adrian ran back in—just in time to see those two birds hot-footing it around the grate then clutching the drawn screen, their wings flapping wildly.

A few minutes later they were curled up in the corner beyond the grate, their beaks opening and closing slowly. Black to begin with, they were now blacker than the electrocuted squirrel that had greeted us on the day we'd moved in. And equally roasted. But I tossed them into my burning pen anyway.

First thing next morning, climbing my extension ladder to the roof above the family room, I capped the flue with a heavy-duty wire screen, making that chimney bird-proof for the duration.

But it was too late. I'd already reconfirmed my status as the cruelest dad ever.

Yard Wars of the Ohio Outback
R2D2

But our first spring on County Road 50 came with inspiring bird moments as well, helping to redeem me in the eyes of my boys.

The first involved hummingbirds, which our neighbor to the west had aplenty because of a trellis of nectar-rich morning glories, where their darting about drove that neighbor's cats crazy. I'd never seen a hummingbird up close before, but one afternoon several zipped by from next door then zipped back just as quickly, at once here—then there—like electrons. I was jealous, of course, because I wanted hummingbirds in *my* yard. I wanted to share their phenomenal flight with Owen and Adrian.

So off I went to Furrows for a hummingbird feeder, a slim plastic tube lined with fake blossoms, each of which had a tiny feeding hole in the center. The instructions said to fill the tube with red sugar-water and hang it in plain sight. So I mixed the red sugar-water, filled the plastic tube, and hung it from the gutter above the Florida room, where the ample expanse of glass offered ready observation.

But that feeder never attracted a single hummingbird. The curious little creatures seemed to prefer the real thing next door—that trellis of nectar-rich morning glories. All we got in *our* yard were ants. Because that plastic tube leaked, producing a red puddle beneath the eaves, as if Owen or Adrian had dropped a cherry popsicle.

The inspiring hummingbird experience was total serendipity, occurring one morning at the picture window in the living room, which I just happened to be passing en route to wind the grandfather clock on the wall beyond. Something flashed at the window. And there it was— if my *Golden Guide to Field Identification of Birds of North America* is to be believed—a ruby-throated hummingbird! It seemed to be inspecting the minnow seine, perhaps having a good laugh at my expense.

I froze in place, hidden by a table lamp in the center of the window, my head above it like an extension of the lampshade, while that hummingbird hovered stock still, staring straight at me, its buzzing wings but a blur. There was nothing to do but stare back, my nose just inches from the glass. And for a few timeless seconds I thought I was costarring in a National Geographic Special. All I could think of was a poem by Emily Dickinson that always confounded the students in my Great Works class, because it never once mentions its subject yet describes a hummingbird so perfectly:

A Route of Evanescence
With a revolving Wheel—
A Resonance of Emerald—
A Rush of Cochineal—
And every Blossom on the Bush
Adjusts its tumbled Head—
The mail from Tunis, probably,
An easy Morning's Ride.

But when I adjusted *my* head to call for Owen and Adrian, that hummingbird fled. And I never saw another.

But I did see bluebirds. And Owen and Adrian and Elaine saw them, too. Because the birdhouse that I'd affixed to the tall metal pipe out back brought bluebirds on the very first try. Bluebirds of happiness! I couldn't believe it, but there they were, confirmed by my binoculars and my *Golden Guide to Field Identification of Birds of North America*—a male and a female, alternately alighting on the little roof of my plywood birdhouse, then flitting off into the cornfield to scratch for food.

One morning during breakfast a magical moment transpired—a

sudden tapping at one of the long narrow windows in the family room, windows overlooking our ball field to the east. One of the bluebirds was fluttering up against the glass. It was the male, in his deep-blue coat and reddish breast, apparently intrigued by the reflection of the rising sun, which simultaneously prevented it from seeing its own reflection as well as anyone who happened to be standing behind the window. Which we all soon were, treated to long minutes of face-to-face bluebird bonding.

"Wow!" Adrian concluded. "It's prettier than those blackbirds you fried!"

Which made Owen laugh. Because he knew it was true.

. . .

The best thing I ever did with the pool that came with our new place was to give it away. Only I wasn't smart enough to do so until the boys were in their teens—when they were more interested in girls and guitars than splashing about in the backyard. But Owen was only in fifth grade when we moved to County Road 50, Adrian in second, and they considered that big round aboveground pool the height of luxury.

I considered it a 24,000-gallon pain in the ass.

The first time I ever saw that pool—when I noticed the HOUSE FOR SALE sign in the front yard and stopped by—it was a hot day in high summer. On a whim I had pulled into the long gravel driveway, parked beside one of the telephone poles, and, when no one answered my knock at the front door, circled the house to the west, to avoid the large black dog barking madly in its pen to the east.

The metal pool was up and running, deliciously inviting on a hot August day. Robin's-egg blue, it had a circular privacy screen rising three feet above the surface, obscuring the owner, who was basking in a chaise longue on the elevated deck. Sunlight sparkled on the surface, and the clear blue water shimmered in disklike bangles all the way to the bottom.

The owner didn't bother to get up to greet me—she could tell someone was coming because of the dog—as I climbed the steps of the ladder to join her aloft.

"Care for a swim?" was all she said. "There are extra swimsuits in the Florida room. You're about the same size as my sons."

I was tempted. But I just stood on that deck for a few minutes, gazing out over the tall corn to the south, all the way to the woodlot on the horizon. And suddenly I saw myself as a country squire. With his very own pool.

The chore facing me now—which became an annual yard war—was to reconcile my vision of the pool on that hot August day with the current reality: a pool with the ladder to the deck locked upright in its winter position, the water drained to one-third of capacity, and a large black cover sagging in the center beneath a puddle of soggy leaves. Moreover, that large black cover was torn and tattered.

The problem was geometrical—a square cover on a round pool—which meant that it had to be crisscrossed and tied down with nylon ropes threaded around and between the stanchions of the privacy screen. In theory, such a cover could be battened down like a snare drum. In practice, as soon as the first good winter wind slipped beneath the overlapping edges, that sucker would inflate like a spinnaker. And subsequent winter winds would rip it to shreds, leaving it whipping in the air like the flag at Fort Henry.

I would witness it again and again in the years to come, each fall believing—as I closed the pool for winter—that I could stretch the new black cover (an annual expense of $125) tighter than ever, running extra nylon rope around the edges where the square cover overlapped the round pool. Each fall I was convinced I could tie it down tighter. But each winter, of course, the first good wind inflated it. Then tore it apart. All it lacked was a skull-and-crossbones to fly like a Jolly Roger over a pirate's bathtub.

So I was in no hurry that first spring to remove the cover and take on the pool. I knew nothing about pools. But Memorial Day was approaching, and Owen and Adrian wanted to swim. They were excited and offered to help.

"OK," I said. "First thing we've got to do is untie all the knots in those yellow ropes." Owen set to work immediately, circling the pool on a mission.

"Put the ladder down, Dad!" Adrian squeaked. "I want to work on the deck!" So I unlatched the ladder, converting it from its upright winter position to its touch-the-ground summer position, and Adrian scrambled aboard. And fell in the pool.

"I couldn't reach the rope!" he explained when we fished him out. Then he ran into the house crying, because Owen was laughing.

Adrian's plunge, which pulled the cover away from the deck, gave us a sneak preview of what lay beneath. I was hoping, of course, to see sparkling clear—albeit shallow—water, needing only an additional 16,000 gallons from the hose. But the pool was one-third filled with what looked like black coffee.

" . . . sunnuvabitch pool!"

"But Dad," Owen pointed out. "You haven't put the chemicals in yet!"

. . .

The little room we called the pool shed extended from the back end of the Florida room like an outhouse. The interior was dark and stank of chlorine.

Unfamiliar pool equipment of all sorts was crammed into that shed—a squat, sand-filled filter ("It looks like R2D2!" Adrian said); ribbed plastic hoses two inches in diameter, to connect the filter to the pool jet and skimmer; circular screw clamps (corroded by their proximity to chemicals during the course of the winter) to hold those hoses in place; a flat vacuum cleaner on the end of a metal pole that extended to twelve feet, to reach the center of the pool from anywhere along the circumference; a flat net like a gigantic fly swatter, for fishing out flotsam and jetsam; a ten-gallon bucket of chlorine pucks; a plastic one-gallon jug of some sort of acid; several quart bottles of algicide; a pH kit; aluminum deck chairs (corroded by their proximity to chemicals during the course of the winter); several quarts of something called Polysheen; a skimmer basket; and half a dozen mousetraps (corroded by their proximity to chemicals during the course of the winter). Of these mousetraps I will have more to say later.

None of the above inventory, as it turned out, was in working order. Moreover, the labels on all of the containers were virtually unreadable, destroyed by chemical action. And none of the containers, of course, was full. Meanwhile, the heady chemical stench—intensified by the May heat—was giving me a whanging headache. So I shut the door to the pool shed and fled into the backyard for a breath of fresh air.

Owen was waiting, having untied most of the knots in the yellow nylon ropes holding down what was left of the pool cover.

"Let's see if we can slip that thing off," I said, "without dumping all those leaves into the pool."

So the two of us tugged from opposite ends on that ragged pool cover, until Owen lost control of his end and it slid from the deck into the water. Dumping the pile of wet leaves into the center of the pool.

"Brown sugar for black coffee!" I said. Which made Owen laugh instead of cry. Then Adrian came back outside, having changed into dry clothes, and I suggested they play badminton. "I'll take care of those leaves myself," I said. "You guys need a break."

So off they went to play badminton, while I went inside to put on my bathing suit. Then, wading about in knee-deep black water, with brown leaf-mush squishing through my toes, I fished out the accumulated crap with the long net, trying all the while to envision the pool as I'd first seen it. But the vision failed.

My first mistake was thinking I could dilute that black water by adding more—living in the country, we had our own well, with an unlimited supply—then clarify it by adding chlorine. So I tossed the hose into the pool and turned it on full blast. Meanwhile, I fussed with the filter, which had to be rolled outside from the pool shed because it was filled with wet sand and too heavy to lift, bumping my head as I wrestled it into place beneath the deck, slicing my fingers as I tightened the clamps on the ribbed plastic hoses.

Two days later, when the pool was filled to the brim, I shocked it with a heavy dose of granular chlorine, tossed a few pucks into the skimmer basket for good measure, and plugged the cord from the filter into the electrical outlet on one of the deck stanchions. Then I scrambled out from under the deck and stood back as R2D2 burbled to life, sucking water from the pool, forcing it through the sand within, and jetting it back, creating a slow counterclockwise motion on the surface. And two days later the black coffee was gone. What we had now was pea soup.

I had no choice but to drain the thing dry and start from scratch.

So I rented a pump from the pool-supply store in Lima and drained the pool, which alienated my neighbor to the east, a divorcée whose teenage son blew grass clippings from their riding mower into our ball field, right through my long line of swamp maple seedlings. The pumped-out pool water—due to the contour of our acre—had made its way into her vegetable garden. Tit for tat.

Then the Memorial Day sun revealed something new—a dull scaly substance coating the plastic liner. This, I was told by the clerk at the pool-supply store in Lima, could easily be dissolved with acid. I tried it, of course, pushing the acid around with a scrub brush affixed to a broom handle—my feet protected by old sneakers, my hands by rubber gloves. But the pungent acid fumes gave me a whanging headache. Without removing a tenth of that white scale.

"We need a new liner," I told Elaine. So I phoned the pool-supply store to order one—installed.

"You should get a new filter while you're at it," said the observant technician who installed the liner. "The one you got isn't gonna last long. Dintcha see that crack?"

No, I hadn't. R2D2 consisted of two hemispheres joined at the equator by a dozen bolts, a hairline crack extending from one of them. Because I'd tightened it too tight.

"Your o-ring's worn as well," the technician said as he dismantled R2D2. "This filter's gonna explode like the space shuttle. Its sand hasn't been changed in years. It cruds up the water. Filter sand should be changed every year."

So we added a brand new filter to the brand new liner. And brand new filter sand. And brand new hoses and brand new clamps and brand new chemicals.

"And why not toss in a brand new pool cover while you're at it?" I said. What the hell. I was a country squire, with my very own pool. I told Elaine I'd cover the expense by teaching summer school.

Then I tossed the hose into the pool and turned it on full blast. And by the end of June, one long month after untying the first knot in the nylon ropes on the tattered cover, the pool looked as it had when I first saw it. And we plunged on in.

The water came up to my waist, Elaine's breasts, Owen's shoulders, and Adrian's chin. I strung the badminton net above the surface, from one side of the privacy screen to the other, and a raucous game of volleyball began.

. . .

The mustard algae appeared a few days later—a cinnamon-like substance that gathered in patches on the bottom of the pool, only to dissolve in a cloud when you tried to vacuum it up. Then settle right back down again.

"It's because your pool's so close to a farm," said the clerk at the pool-supply store. "I have just what you need." (He always did.) A quart of algicide.

But the stuff did no good, although it did kill that algae. The resulting algae corpses were finer than dust—so fine that, when vacuumed up, they blew right through the sand in the new filter (R2D2 Jr.) and jetted back into the pool. To settle down again like cinnamon.

The daily pool maintenance, of course, fell to me—cleaning the skimmer basket, netting the flotsam and jetsam, vacuuming the bottom, inserting the chlorine pucks, testing the pH, hosing the deck, setting out the aluminum furniture, tightening the badminton net, picking up towels and volleyballs—demanding hours of my time. The mustard algae was just one more nuisance.

"OK," I kept telling myself. "We can live with that, we can live with that."

But what we couldn't live with were the insidious insects that descended on the pool each summer, each in its own month, as if on cue.

The swim-dive bugs came in June—gray cigar-shaped creatures an inch in length with two whiplike appendages for wings. They appeared in the water as soon as we opened the pool, swimming along on the surface, then abruptly diving like submarines. Hence the name bestowed on them by Owen and Adrian.

"They're fun to catch!" Adrian said, holding one in his cupped hands. Then it stung him in the palm and he ran inside crying. Those swim-dive bugs were vicious. I took great delight in scooping them from the surface in the long flat net, turning the net over to pin them on the deck, and squishing them one by one with a jab of my finger.

But the biting flies, which appeared in July, were impossible to catch. These looked exactly like regular flies except for their transparent wings, which bore a small black dot in the center like a bull's-eye. They acted like dive-bombers, attacking me whether I was swimming in the pool or mowing the grass. Like mosquitoes, they were attracted to perspiration. But unlike mosquitoes—which you had the pleasure of smacking after you were bitten—they were unsmackable. When you were swimming they liked to land on your wet head, where you couldn't feel them until you'd been nailed. And by the time you'd slapped yourself, of course, they were gone. *Bite! Ow! Slap!*

"Goddam sunnuvabitch flies!"

But the absolute worst were the horseflies. Which were enormous.

Many Ohio insects, in fact, were larger than their cousins in other states. The ladybugs were twice the size of those I'd caught as a kid in Connecticut. And the fireflies were as big as horseflies. The Ohio horseflies, in turn, were as big as hummingbirds. Maybe, like the mustard algae, it had something to do with the proximity of farms, where they could feed on manure and mutate. Whatever the reason, they were malicious. They'd appear out of nowhere, buzz your head, touch the surface of the pool for a quick drink, then buzz off in crazy zig-zag flight.

One morning, after finishing my pool maintenance chores, I lay down on the warm metal deck and bent an arm across my face to shield my eyes from the sun. Seconds later one of those hummingbird-size horseflies zipped by, bit me on the upper lip, and zipped off.

"The bite from the larger specimens of horsefly can be painful," the head of the Biology Department told me. "Their mandibles are like serrated scimitars. They slice the flesh, causing it to swell."

Leaving my lip looking like the thumb of a boxing glove.

New Stark, Breathless

PRAY FOR RAIN is the plea one area farmer has mowed in large letters across his fields, to make certain it is visible from on high. Area churches have held prayer services. The last good rain—1.2 inches—fell on Easter Sunday. Since then there have been two or three false alarms—much wind, with dark clouds and thunder and lightning, and scattered raindrops amounting to less than a tenth of an inch. The unfaithful have sponsored an Indian rain dance, with no success. Others talk of seeding the clouds. But there are no clouds to seed. Rainfall is off ten inches.

"God's testing our character," Bill Rausch's wife tells him. The Rausches farm a thousand acres around New Stark, a family enterprise that dates back 100 years. Bill grew up in New Stark, and his mother, who is seventy-six, recently said to him, "There's nothing I can tell you about the weather now. You've seen it all." Marjorie Marquart's mother is ninety-one and can't remember it any worse.

The heat is relentless, with a palpable presence. New Stark bakes and swelters. The grass is the color of straw; the trees are shedding leaves in self-defense. In the surrounding fields, which stretch away in all directions, the corn stands crippled, half the height it should be, and the soybeans languish, ankle deep. Dark clumps of trees dot the horizon, wrapped by the gauze of a shimmering haze.

The heat wave began the third weekend in May, when it turned ninety-five degrees overnight, and temperature records have been broken almost daily since. June was clear and bright, but July has turned hazy. It was 104 when I stopped in New Stark on Friday, July 8, 1988. I stopped on a whim, struck by a sense of history. There is a certain grim satisfaction in knowing that what you are experiencing is the worst it's ever been.

Also, I wanted to learn about the Lincoln Highway. The year 1988 marked the seventy-fifth anniversary of this antique national route, a road constructed through Ohio along old Indian trails, to join San Francisco and New York via Chicago. A commemorative tour, led by California highway historian Lyn Protteau, left New York on June 11 and soon passed through, further contributing to the historical significance of New Stark's summer. According to Protteau, "It is quite probable that the Lincoln Highway played an enormous part in the development of America's economy, establishing the importance of good roads, and making the automobile practical and affordable."

Finally, I stopped in New Stark because I wanted to know if its name was in any way related to the landscape.

. . .

U.S. Route 30, the old Lincoln Highway, is a two-lane road. It's one of the best in Ohio and, as the truckers will tell you, the shortest direct east-west route. The speed limit is fifty-five miles per hour, and the trucks—huge Mack rigs with sleek airfoils above their cabs and ROADWAY or CAROLINA or some other logo painted broadside on their trailers—blow through at seventy. At that speed, you have less than fifteen seconds to see New Stark. But there isn't very much to see. Nine bungalow-style homes hug the quarter-mile strip between two green-and-white metal signs that announce the village. Three of these houses sit vacant, although it's difficult to tell when driving by. There are two mobile homes: one empty, the other closed up, its owners on vacation. The two grandest structures are in disrepair: a gutted church of white clapboards with a tall belfry above the arched front door and a ten-room, two-story frame house, scarcely visible through a jungle of trees and brush that encase it like a diseased skin. Another dilapidated structure—a two-story frame building of gray clapboards—leans against its one-story addition of yellow brick. Beside it stands a weathered, peaked garage made of vertical boards. U.S. Route 30 is intersected in the center of New Stark by Van Buren Township Road 61, a narrow road that runs south several miles to the Hancock County line and dead-ends to the north in the ravaged fields.

But let me take you on a walking tour, retracing my steps as I discovered New Stark. I arrived from the west, parking on the south side of the highway, just inside the New Stark sign, along a gravel berm that runs for about 100 yards. This shoulder is the widest segment of Route 30 for miles, the only decent place to park or turn around. Elsewhere in the village the road comes right to the edge of the straw-colored yards, and along the fields the berm is virtually nonexistent, giving way immediately to deep ditches. Yellow lines with cat's-eyes mark the center of the highway, and unbroken white lines define the edge.

Route 30 is well maintained (sections near New Stark were repaved last summer), and the asphalt is thick and smooth. There are no potholes, but the road is dangerous. Every driveway has room enough for two vehicles to turn around so the locals don't have to back into traffic. I sat in my car for ten minutes before mustering the courage to get out, daunted by the whoosh of passing trucks. Then I crunched my way along the berm, through chunks of rubber and the carcasses of animals.

Just outside of New Stark I had seen a doe and her fawn, freshly killed. The animals get struck and killed, then struck again and flattened, then struck again and shunted to the roadside where, when the birds and broiling sun have done their work, they can be identified only by the color of their fur. I saw a brown squirrel, a black skunk, and a calico cat. As Bill Rausch's daughter Susie says, "In New Stark you get used to losing your pets."

But the loss of human life is the real tragedy. Marjorie Marquart, who's lived in New Stark since 1943, tells of a woman in a VW that went under a semi. She was extricated in pieces. Another collision between a car and two semis left a leg in one front yard. The worst occurred when a truck ran into a school bus from behind. Bill Rausch and his wife hunted for the bodies of the children in the soybean field across from their farmhouse. Recently, not far from New Stark, a semi plowed into a home, pinning a woman under her bed for hours. The incident has revived a rallying cry: *Widen the berm!* But the attendant politics move slowly. The Lincoln Highway is supposed to be expanded to four lanes, but, as anyone in New Stark will tell you, that kind of talk has been heard for years, and the starting date is always a decade away. In rural areas you just have to wait.

To the right of the gravel berm is a half-acre lot overgrown with Queen Anne's lace, goldenrod, and a stalky green weed with pale blue flowers. The rusted T-shaped overhang once sheltered gasoline pumps. The broken refrigerator case and Toledo scales are from a subsequent fruit stand. An abandoned Jeeplike vehicle and a Chevrolet sit farther back among some trees. And if you hunt around in there, you might find the remains of a tennis court.

But if you just stand in the lot and wait for the traffic to thin, the whoosh of trucks will disappear, and New Stark will suddenly turn silent, as silent as the white cottonwood seeds sailing overhead on the hot prairie breeze. Then you'll hear birds—although you can't see them. Noisy tweeting plus a strange *ooh* sound that is either an owl or a mourning dove. Then that numbing summer loneliness that Huck Finn speaks of overwhelms you.

For me the spell wasn't broken until someone stepped from the mobile home in the lot across the highway, and suddenly I was no longer the only one outside in the 104-degree July heat of New Stark.

The attractive mobile home sits endwise to the highway on the first lot at the edge of the fields. A stand of trees separates it from the next lot, where a modular ranch built in 1981 waits for 100 pounds of grass seed to emerge from the acre of brown dirt that surrounds it. The Neelys, who have lived in New Stark for only a year and a half, are afraid to use their well to water the seed. Out back is a satellite dish, and further along a large black barn, the kind that, in other parts of the country, would say CHEW MAIL POUCH TOBACCO. In front of the barn is a rusty mobile home that the Neelys are refurbishing, hoping to rent it out on the next lot up, which they also own. Crossing the highway, I call to the person leaving the first trailer, a lanky youth wearing only cutoff jeans. He is the Neelys' "adopted runaway" son, and he takes me through the trees to his home next door.

Inside, the only central air conditioning system in New Stark hits me like a hammer. It takes my eyes a moment to adjust to the interior darkness. Mrs. Neely is curled up on the sofa; her husband, who retired early with a disability, is in the recliner, feet up. They are watching a movie from the satellite on a four-foot-square television screen. Being newcomers, they're afraid they can't tell me much about New Stark. The property with the mobile home had belonged to friends who went bankrupt. The Neelys bought it to help them out, renting it to relatives. Then their own house came on the market through a sheriff's sale. It had replaced an old home destroyed by arson. Years ago the property had held the Gilbert Candy Company; then a hay dealer named Stager put up a barn. Stager sold it to Spears, who used the barn for painting buses. Then Spears sold it to Hanna, who got burned out and couldn't make payments on the modular replacement. So the Neelys took over. In addition, they are buying the scrubby field along the berm where I parked my car. They also dickered for property near the village, but the owner, who had bought it on speculation that the highway would be widened, wanted too much—$3,000 an acre, when farmland is going for $800.

"Maybe someday this place will be called 'Neelyville,'" Mrs. Neely laughs. They don't know why it's called New Stark. Guess it was named for somebody named Stark. "What's it like living out here?" I ask. "Quiet," says the adopted runaway son. The Neelys have two grown sons of their own. They tell me about the truckers that overturn in the soybean fields, truckers that come in to use the phone, truckers "broke down" from blowouts or other problems. "It gets cold out there in the winter," Mrs. Neely says. "We're always glad to help." She's going to ask their councilman if the speed limit can be reduced to forty-five through the village, if she can find out who their councilman is.

But to learn about New Stark, Mr. Neely says, I ought to talk to Old Man Coleman, next house up the road. He's lived in New Stark for twenty-five years. He's on vacation now, but his daughter's looking after the house, a tidy place painted beige and brown, with an L-shaped front porch.

The front windows are open, the steamy air rustling the Swiss-dot curtains, and though I can tell that the Colemans' daughter is in there, she doesn't answer when I knock on the screen door.

· · ·

About the only positive effect of the drought is that the mosquito population has dwindled. After the previous summer's rains, an entomologist estimated that there were 500,000 mosquitoes in Ohio *per capita*. This summer I have not encountered a single mosquito in New Stark. But experts are predicting a mosquito explosion as soon as eggs hatch in the cracks and crevices of dried-up creeks and riverbeds. Birds that feed on mosquitoes are in danger, as are fish in the depleted streams. Scattered fish kills have been reported. Meanwhile, worms are in short supply for fishermen. The price of a dozen Canadian nightcrawlers has doubled.

Bee stings are also down this summer. Flowers aren't growing, so bees can't get nectar. As a result, the fall honey crop will suffer. All wildlife seems confused. Squirrels can't find nuts to store. Raccoons are abandoning their young—I saw one such orphan in a dry stand of trees not far from New Stark—and the deer are ranging wide in search of water. The deer will survive, experts say—if they can avoid the traffic when they cross the Lincoln Highway. But lack of a historical database for such severe conditions makes it virtually impossible to predict the effect.

Early Saturday morning it is ninety-four degrees in the shade on the thermometer at Elgene Neiswander's. Elgene's thermometer is from a filling station that used to be in the peaked garage down the street. So New Stark once had *two* gas stations, side by side along the gravel berm. The thermometer is at least three feet tall and says PRESTONE DOES NOT BOIL AWAY, although this summer just might be the exception.

But I begin my second day in New Stark back at the Colemans' place, and once again the daughter does not answer, though I walk the L-shaped porch and call through the curtains. Discouraged, I head east up the highway.

On the adjacent lot, which the Colemans own, is an abandoned bungalow with green-shingle siding. Next comes the intersection of Van Buren Township 61, then another abandoned house—white with a drab tin roof—behind a broken wall of stones. This used to be the post office, when New Stark merited the mail.

At the next place I get lucky—Dallas and Alice Cheney are at home, their grandson watching Saturday-morning cartoons. Their living room is a comfortable clutter of old, unmatched furniture. Dallas, who is retired, laughs out loud when I tell him I'm interested in New Stark. Alice has lived here for thirty-one years.

"Why do they call it New Stark?" I ask.

"Cuz you have to be stark-ravin' mad to live here!" Dallas says.

On the wall above the television is a portrait of an Indian. Area farmers are forever turning up arrowheads in their fields. The prehistoric Ohio Indians were the Mound Builders. Later tribes—the Shawnee, Wyandot, Miami, Seneca, Ottawa, Delaware, and Mingo—were sent west to reservations 150 years ago, about the time that New Stark was founded. There are graphic tales of Indian torture and executions, and, as a local historian says, "These accounts dispel any romantic notions we may have about Indians and make clear the dangers of the wilderness." No mistaking where sympathies lay back then.

The Cheneys' place is next to the gutted church. "We own it," Dallas says. The cornerstone says 1892. First it was the Presbyterian, then Baptist, New Stark Faith Chapel. It has stood vacant for twelve years. The Cheneys couldn't afford it when it first came up for sale, so an out-of-towner bought it and sold off the pews. Then kids shot out the windows with BB guns. Dallas hopes to lower the ceilings in the old structure and use it for storage. Or else raze it and create elbow room next door.

A strange contraption leans against the side of the church, something that looks like the *Gossamer Albatross* without wings. "Gyrocoptor," Dallas says. He got it from a manufacturer in Muncie, Indiana. "NASA built 'em for observation," he explains, "but the engine was too small." He's planning to fix it up for the grandchildren.

From Alice I learn that the old building with the yellow-brick addition is the Cherry Tree Antique Shop, New Stark's only business. The trucks have blown the sign down. Margie West has run the shop for twenty years. She's English and doesn't live in the village. Before Margie, that old place had been a general store. You could get anything over there, Alice says—groceries, hardware, dry goods. Most of all she remembers the "huckster wagon," an old truck that made the rounds from the store every Friday. You went in one end and came out the other. There was penny candy and ice cream. The kids loved it. "And that big old house across the street—you can only see the roof above the trees and wild bushes—my mother once told me it was the Baughman Hotel." Alice pauses as if in disbelief. "People used to say New Stark was popular."

While we're talking, Alice writes out a list of names. Marjorie Marquart, Solomon's widow, lives in the little house beyond the church; she's been here the longest, forty-five years. Elgene Neiswander— white-brick house across the highway—forty-two years. Bill Rausch is on the farm at the east end of the village. He grew up in this house. The house beyond the Marquarts' is empty.

Marquart, Neiswander, Rausch—all German, in accord with a 1910 history of Van Buren Township I turned up in Lima overnight: "German immigrants, industrious, thrifty, honest and moral, their robust health the result of frugal living, and their solid strength backed up by a fixed determination to succeed in the land of their adoption, soon opened up valuable farms, and today we have not a more industrious, peaceable and contented people in the township."

Marjorie Marquart isn't home, but across the highway at the white-brick house I catch Elgene Pore Neiswander drawing her bath. Years ago, she says, New Stark was all Pores—Maud Pore, Paul Pore, Uncle Cloyce—but it's nothing like it was. You don't know the people anymore. There's still the New Stark Social Circle, but nobody from New Stark belongs. Elgene was widowed by her first husband and divorced by her second, who got fancy ideas about women off the television. "Did you know," she says with an air of surprise, "you can get a divorce just by living apart for a year?" Elgene lives with her son, a truck driver. The interior walls of her house are just plaster over brick, so it gets ice cold in winter. The place is heated by fuel oil, kerosene, and a wood-burning stove. Out back the American flag floats from a pole on the garage, although it's the ninth of July. Fireworks were banned on the Fourth because of dryness.

Elgene shows me the trees in her yard. She planted them herself. There are more trees in New Stark than you notice from the highway. A lot of walnut and buckeye and ragged weeping willows. It's just the wide fields and high sky that make it seem empty.

"Why do they call it New Stark?" I ask Elgene.

"Because the people came from Stark County over east," she says.

Her husband's granddad came from there, about 100 miles as the crow flies. But she doesn't know how Stark County got its name.

And the Lincoln Highway? When her first husband was little, Elgene recalls, the children used to play in the road. Can you believe it? Today, the trucks knock your house down while you sleep. But wait a minute. Elgene goes into the house and fetches me a newspaper clipping, a marvelous reminiscence of New Stark in the early days of the Lincoln Highway. It is by the Reverend Marlon R. Thomas, grandson of the Baughmans, who owned the large abandoned house next door to Elgene's.

The highway was proposed in 1912, Thomas writes, and the Lincoln Highway Association was formed in 1913. At first the road was "piked"—spread with crushed stone to render it passable—then paved with concrete. The asphalt came later. Thomas calls the Lincoln Highway the "Atlantic-to-Pacific-across-the-nation Main Street to America," and his grandparents' big old home was right on it.

"Grandma put up lovely, colorful cloth awnings about her huge home windows, refurbished her many bedrooms in style, put up a neat and attractive ROOMS FOR RENT sign in the front lawn, and many customers who drove the Lincoln Highway year after year stayed in New Stark, with an excellent breakfast served before they left. We could visit with people from all across America in days when that was a high privilege."

Thomas waxes poetic about his grandpa's horseless carriage with the flapping side curtains, the music from the old Edison, and life in New Stark by the light of a coal-oil lamp. "Our people came to the area in 1836 and from then on began to clear the farmlands. Brethren and Mennonite people came down the old Indian trail, which became the Lincoln Highway, from Stark County and called their home 'New Stark.'"

. . .

Sunday morning. The day is hot and grainy. The car radio forecasts rain. But we've heard that one before. A "yellow alert" is in effect. Polluted air, trapped by the stifling heat wave, is causing health problems. The Ohio EPA adds an ozone warning. If this is the greenhouse effect, I want out. Mandatory water conservation measures will go into effect this week at surrounding municipalities, since voluntary measures have not been working. Truckloads of hay from Virginia and North Carolina are arriving for area dairy farmers. Migrant workers in neighboring counties fear there won't be enough tomatoes and cucumbers on the vine to earn them a ticket home. Senator Howard Metzenbaum (D-Ohio) is opposing a proposal to divert Great Lakes water into the Mississippi. He claims it's illegal. Finally, the straw-colored grass is just dormant, not yet dead. So much for the news.

In New Stark Margie West is refinishing furniture at the Cherry Tree Antique Shop. I can hardly see her in there through the crusty plateglass windows of the old general store. A wooden case of Pepsi-Cola bottles sits on a dusty shelf in the dim interior. Margie doesn't have much time to talk. She is preparing for a show in Columbus. She unlocks the rusty chain from within and steps out to greet me, closing the double doors in her dogs' faces. Once, when her dogs got out, they were all killed by the traffic within minutes. Their replacements are small and not very vicious. "But they bark," Margie says.

The trucks are rolling by within inches of my back, swirling bits of straw into my face. I can hardly hear Margie speak. "Tell me about your place!" I shout.

Margie is about seventy, a year or two older than most women in New Stark—all business in her dirty apron. She is from Yorkshire, England, and served with the admiralty during the war. The shop's really not open to the public anymore, she says—except for her regular customers—so it doesn't matter that the trucks blew the sign down. Margie's a purist, only dealing in antiques before 1835. She does all of her work on the premises.

"Handwritten deeds to the property date to 1835," Margie says. "The store was built in 1865." The yellow-brick addition used to house a Model T dealership. A sawmill, a chicken hatchery, and a dairy were also on the property. Margie bought the place in the early sixties, when supermarkets put the general store under.

I ask her what she thinks of the old Baughman place. "It was ruined before they let it sit and rot," she says. "They lowered the ceilings inside." She makes it sound worse than the time she was robbed. Two men walked into the shop one day, and it was obvious they hadn't come for antiques. They demanded money. When Margie resisted, they beat her up, took her purse, and left her for dead. A neighbor saw them fleeing and came to Margie's aid.

I can tell Margie wants to get back to work, so I excuse myself when the Colemans' daughter comes out to look for the Sunday paper. But by the time I have crossed the highway, she has scuttled back into the house.

Undaunted, I make it to the east end of the village just in time to catch Marjorie Marquart coming home from church. She is dressed in her summer finery and is holding a thick, black Bible. "I saw you around," she says, and suddenly I realize how conspicuous I have been, walking up and down the highway, notebook in hand, while the folks of New Stark have been minding their own business, inside and out of the heat.

The Marquart home is the oldest in New Stark, built in 1873. The interior is neat and clean. Large floor fans push the hot air around. The sign on the wall says WELCOME FRIENDS. Marjorie has lived in New Stark longer than any current resident—forty-five years. Anticipating my visit, she has made notes and laid out a map. Van Buren Township is one of seventeen in Hancock County. Like the state with its eighty-eight counties, the seventeen townships make a rough square grid. Hancock County, formed in 1820, was named for John Hancock, signer of the Declaration of Independence.

Marjorie's late husband was the township supervisor for thirty-three years, which meant he built the roads, mowed the grass, and plowed the snow. "Snow on Sunday, blow on Monday," her husband used to say. Marjorie recalls the winter of 1945, when her husband plowed snow every day from December to February. When it finally stopped snowing, he took her outside and showed her a gouge left by a bulldozer—at the top of a telephone pole.

Marjorie speaks fondly of New Stark, "a thriving town years ago." There was a creamery, a barbershop, and a restaurant. Once a week people came "from far and near" for a trap shoot in the field behind the general store. Marjorie would like to see the folks in the village get together now once a year, but she doesn't think it will ever happen. She can remember when there were thirty-four children in New Stark. Most attended a one-room schoolhouse just outside the village, which was also the site of New Stark String College—"Don't ask me why they called it that," she laughs—where teachers could take the "normal course." For a rural area, Marjorie points out, New Stark has produced its share of professional people—doctors, dentists, lawyers, teachers, and an entomologist. There simply wasn't enough land for all the kids to make a life of farming, so education was encouraged.

Marjorie is a new breed of senior citizen. A semi-retired LPN, she works at the nearest McDonald's. "You get old quick if you don't keep busy," she says. She owns twelve acres behind her little house, land she rents to an area farmer. This summer it's planted in wheat, the only crop that has managed to survive. An early crop, the wheat was recently harvested, then the stalks were cut for straw, hence the yellow stuff blowing about the highway. Around New Stark, the wheat fields look almost normal—large golden squares amid the withered corn and soybeans and the diverted acres that have been left to ragged weeds.

"Tell me about Route 30."

"It's a deathtrap," Marjorie says. "I wish they'd move it."

And we talk on through the afternoon. Then a storm warning is issued. Hail and high winds are predicted. It looks like it might rain after all. This just might be the day. The sky has turned black, and the trees—as if in appeal—have turned up their silvery undersides. Expecting the worst, I head back to Lima, but not before arranging to meet Bill Rausch at his farm tomorrow.

Later that evening, thunder begins to roll and lightning rips the sky. There is no hail, but high winds blow the corn flat. In my imagination I am staying at the old Baughman place, looking at the Lincoln Highway from my rented room. And then it rains—for all of five minutes. Another false alarm in New Stark.

· · ·

Monday, July 11, is my last day in New Stark. I spend it with the Rausches—across the highway from Marjorie Marquart's—where the farm pond has dropped two feet since spring. Its surface is littered with leaves from last night's storm. A large black mongrel called Caesar greets me with fangs bared, but his tail is wagging. "He won't hurt you," the Rausches' daughter calls. And she is right.

Bill Rausch has been out in the fields, pulling weeds by hand, because the herbicides haven't dissolved in the soil. He's paying his teenage son and his friend to help him. "I offered 'em half the crop," he jokes, "but they want cash instead."

The corn somehow seems taller today, even after the brief rain. "It's unwrapped," Bill explains. Corn wraps itself like a mummy to hide from the heat. How bad is the drought? "In New Stark? It's worse than you hear." Bill has a farmer friend who recently got back from a trip through Indiana and Illinois, where the corn still has a chance. But in New Stark it's shot. A disaster. "You can't even use it for silage," Bill says, "because of the nitrates. Nothing to do but plow it under." The drought will cost Bill Rausch $150,000, and it'll take him two to three years of hard work to make that up.

His soybeans, however, might make it—if it rains soon. Like today. Like *right now*. The Rausches' soybeans go to Pioneer, one of the world's largest seed companies, as a seed crop for next year's planting. But Pioneer is already renting out land in Argentina, where the seasons are opposite ours, to plant soybeans so there will be seed for next spring.

"I'm not going to get depressed and blow my head off," Bill says. "I used the best seed. I planted well. I don't know what I'd rather be doing."

He's already had his banker out for a look at the fields. "I told him to bring his truck," Bill laughs. "'What truck?' he said. The truck you'll need to farm this place, because I can't pay you." Bill's worried because his bank is now based in Cincinnati, where they don't know farming. "People here pay their bills," he says proudly. "But not this year."

I mention what I heard on the radio driving over, that the federal government will provide aid in the form of low-interest loans—only 4.5 percent. "We don't need a loan," Bill says. "We need a grant."

When he gets going on the government, Bill Rausch sounds like Huck Finn's father. "Jimmy Carter was a farmer, but he bankrupted himself while in office and never knew it until he went home. We've got to get rid of the surpluses," he says adamantly. "And the embargoes—they kill us. They lose our accounts. The government likes to keep food cheap. Food's always used as a tool to manipulate. If we ever get a farmers' union, watch out. We'll be worse than the teamsters, *without* the Mafia. We'll control food!"

Then Bill tells me about growing up in New Stark—which, as my Sunday-night research revealed, is ultimately named for General John Stark, hero of the Battle of Bennington in the Revolutionary War—and about how hard it was for him to lie awake on summer nights, listening to the *clink clink* of horseshoes down the road by the hardware store. That's where all the action was, but it was "men only." Dad's night out at Mel's. That's what the place was called. Mel's. There were gasoline pumps out front. So New Stark once had *three* gas stations, all in a row.

Then there was the time Bill's mother sent him to the store for a jar of mayonnaise and he dropped it in the road. He was afraid to go home, and he can still see that hunk of mayonnaise sitting there in the middle of the Lincoln Highway. People were more trusting then, he says. But today. . . .

I slap at the flies biting my legs—I have been wearing shorts, like everyone else in New Stark, because of the heat—but the flies don't seem to bother Bill Rausch. Or his wife and son, who come out to join us on the porch. Maybe it's the residue of aftershave from yesterday—I put on aftershave to visit Marjorie Marquart. But flies or no, I'm in no hurry to move from the wooden bench I share with Bill Rausch, though it's not the most comfortable seat in the world. So I just keep swatting flies and chewing the fat in New Stark, where the drought and the heat continue unabated as the huge trucks blow by on Route 30, and where the sunsets—oh boy, the sunsets—are as long and red as the stripes on Old Glory.

Yard Wars of the Ohio Outback

Antiseptic

Toward the end of August those hummingbird-size horseflies began to alight on the side of the house to mate. That's when I launched a counterattack to exact my revenge.

I'd been puzzled by two flyswatters that the previous owner had left hanging from small nails in the Florida room—one yellow, one red—each a square of tough plastic affixed to a long wire handle. But now I knew exactly what those were for. Swatting horseflies. The previous owner had two sons, and I was convinced that the flyswatters had been theirs, left behind expressly for me to now issue them to Owen and Adrian, like muskets to militiamen.

"See those big black buggers on the side of the house?" I said, extending a flyswatter in each hand. "I'll give you a penny for every one you kill."

"We'll make a million!" Owen said.

"I want the red one!" Adrian said, swapping his weapon with Owen.

They were delighted with their mission. And black smudges soon dotted the green panel siding. But I didn't mind. The house was ten years old and needed to be repainted—my end-of-summer chore after summer school. By which time Owen and Adrian had killed horseflies by the hundreds, initiating an annual sport that, in the matter of a few years, substantially reduced the horsefly population in our yard. I didn't think such a thing was possible, but the head of the Biology Department confirmed it.

It was the best few bucks I ever spent.

. . .

Before I could paint the house, however, I had to engage in another round of trench warfare. And by now—having dug a long trench for telephone poles across the entire backyard—I was an expert in trench warfare, which seemed the only solution to a new and complicated problem.

The previous owner didn't want ditches out front. So she'd hired a man to tile them shut, bulldozing the yard level with the road. But the ditches were the property of Hardin County, and filling them in was a violation of the law. So the County engineers had ordered the tiling dug up and the ditches restored.

Annoyed at having to undo what he'd just done, the hired man with the bulldozer had done it hastily, leaving a dishlike depression in the west side of the front yard, right along the property line. I remember the previous owner warning me about this, but in our enthusiasm at moving in I'd forgotten the ramifications—ramifications that would be rammed into my brain every time it rained. Because rainwater remained in that depression, creating a mud hole in which mosquitoes bred, yellow jackets nested, and wild fescue grew knee-high—a situation made worse by the fact that it was fed by the leech field of our septic system.

Two cement covers to the septic tank protruded from the ground in front of the large swamp maple to the rear of our badminton court. Four gravel-filled subterranean trenches extended from this tank like parallel fingers. The previous owner had sketched me a map on the back of an envelope, showing their approximate location.

Given the contour of our lot, this leech field drained quite naturally toward the ditch out front and the property line to the west, contributing a constant supply of effluent to that mud hole and making the grass there grow four times faster than anywhere else in the yard.

That's one reason why I never considered a riding mower on County Road 50. All our neighbors had riding mowers—and pickup trucks in which to transport them for servicing—plus a separate push mower for mowing their ditches. But you couldn't mow a mud hole with a riding mower. It'd sink right in. Nor would a riding mower fit into the trunk of the Nova.

Residents of Hardin County weren't required to maintain their ditches, however, since the property belonged to the county, which mowed them once or twice a season, sending out a worker on a tractor with a sidearm flail of the sort you see mowing the embankments of the interstates. The rest of the time the ditches looked like hell, laced with weeds, wildflowers, and litter—unless you maintained them yourself.

Given my golf shoes, Lawn Boy, and practice with our steep yard in Virginia, mowing the ditches was no problem for me. But mowing that mud hole was. The tall grass clogged the Lawn Boy, and the Lawn Boy, in turn, churned up the mud. Which is why it became imperative to fill in what was rapidly becoming, in the course of that rainy spring, a miniature version of the Great Black Swamp. Right in our front yard.

I attacked the problem by shoveling gravel from the driveway into my wheelbarrow, trundling it back and forth, and dumping it into that mud hole, which sucked it up like quicksand. It was obvious that something more substantial was needed to absorb the muck. So I trucked my wheelbarrow into the cornfield and skimmed dirt from between the rows, making trip after trip, overfilling that mud hole until it resembled a gigantic pitcher's mound. I didn't plant grass but left it open to the air, hoping it would dry up more quickly. But it didn't.

"It looks awful," Elaine said.

"It'll look better when the ground settles."

But the ground wouldn't settle. So the rain ran off to the side, threatening to create another mud hole beside the pitcher's mound— another quagmire and quandary. It was maddening. Until the old eggbeater started whirring.

"I'll dig a trench out to the ditch," I told Elaine, "and make a drain to carry away the excess water."

"We're out of Gatorade," she said.

"I'll get some on my way home from Furrows." Where I purchased a ten-yard-long coil of five-inch-wide perforated black plastic drainage tile, wedging it into the trunk of the Nova.

But all I had to guide me in this battle plan was a map of the four subterranean trenches of the leech field hastily sketched on the back of an envelope by the previous owner. My idea was to dig another trench—between the fourth one of the leech field and the pitcher's mound—to relieve the pressure on the latter once I'd tiled it out to the ditch.

I began by cutting out the grass with an edger and stacking the turf to the side. Then I dug the trench with a round-pointed shovel, making it exactly as wide as the blade of the shovel itself. Before long, piles of gray clay paralleled the stacked turf in a neat line toward the ditch.

I worked hard throughout the afternoon. And then, just before sundown, my shovel produced a strange sound. A clanky sort of crunch. I'd hit gravel. Seconds later a thin black watery substance began to ooze—then gush—into the long gray trench. This caused my imagination to flee to something I'd seen returning from Furrows, when I'd taken a different route home in search of Gatorade. I'd never noticed it before—a historical marker dedicated to a man by the name of Faurot who'd discovered oil near the Ottawa River in 1885, making Lima, for a brief time, and quite incredibly, the oil capital of the entire world.

"Oil!" I yelled to Elaine. "I've struck oil!"

Then the deep hot stench of a hundred outhouses stung my nostrils.

It wasn't oil, of course. I'd been digging right over the fourth finger to the leech field, the contents of which were now flooding through my trench—draining all four fingers in rapid succession into the roadside ditch. It was impossible to stop, despite my pathetic attempt at shoveling in clay. All I could do was stand back and clasp a handkerchief to my face.

The rainy spring had filled that leech field to capacity. Now its pungent efflux was en route to Lake Erie.

. . .

By dawn, the ditch along the road had run dry, so I refilled the trench with clay and carefully replaced the turf. No one saw me except the curious cats from next door, distracted from their hummingbird vigil.

By the time I finished you couldn't tell that I'd been there. The west side of our front yard—except for the pitcher's mound—was as neat as if I'd hired Jim Massillo. The only telltale sign of what had transpired was a black swath along the bottom of our ditch, dwindling to a thin black stripe the farther it went. Breezes from the west had carried off the stench under cover of darkness.

Fortunately, our ditches drained to the east, and our divorced neighbor to the east was on vacation with her teenage son—the one who blew grass clippings into our yard with their riding mower—sparing me any questions or confrontation about the black stripe in their ditch. Beyond their place the ditch turned north, crossing beneath County Road 50 in a large corrugated pipe to continue along the border of the Allens' acreage on its way to Grass Run.

So I was back to square one. Meanwhile, Elaine had joined me out front. Owen and Adrian were still asleep, exhausted from hunting horseflies.

"What'll you do with that?" Elaine said, nodding at the coiled tile.

"Return it to Furrows."

"And the ugly mound?"

I was silent for a moment. Then the old eggbeater started whirring. "Plant our Christmas tree there in December. It'll absorb moisture and help the ground sink!"

But it was only August—the dog days—and I'd had enough of this particular yard war. So I declared a truce with the pitcher's mound, sowing it with grass seed to prevent potential mudslides.

"Farmers are always finding arrowheads in the fields around here," I told Elaine. "We can say it's an Indian burial mound."

I picked up grass seed at Furrows when returning the tile, purchasing paint and paintbrushes to boot, hoping to get the house painted before the start of the school year. I never expected the counterattack that followed. But suddenly the driveway—seriously thinned of its gravel to fill the mud hole—began to sport weeds in all the bare spots. Dandelions, clover, and chickweed had moved right in, creating an eyesore.

Goddam sunnuvabitch weeds!

That long gray gravel driveway was essential to my self-concept as a country squire. All country estates have such driveways. They exude a fresh, clean smell after a rain. And announce visitors with a pleasant crunch. It's a happy sound, different from the noiseless asphalt we'd had in Virginia, which required annual blacktopping. Or the concrete on Christopher Circle, which was cracking by the time we moved. The only trouble with a gravel driveway is that it'll grow weeds if you borrow its gravel.

In need of reinforcements, I perused the Yellow Pages and called a quarry near Lima.

"What size gravel you want?" said the woman who answered.

"Don't know," I said. "Driveway size."

"In general, the 6–10 millimeter gravels are used for footpaths. The 10–18 are for driveways. It's a matter of personal taste."

But I didn't know the size of the gravel in our driveway. And I wasn't about to go out and measure. The only ruler I had in the house was in inches—not millimeters—and I didn't know how to convert the one to the other.

"The smaller the gravel," the woman continued, "the more cats like to use it as a toilet."

"Let's go with 18 millimeters," I said. "There are cats next door."

"How much you need?"

I gave her the dimensions of the driveway, and two days later an enormous dump truck appeared out front, the sort you see at major construction sites.

Of course, the driver of that dump truck faced the same problem as the driver of the moving van in the spring: how to avoid the ditches while backing into the driveway to unload his load. But I was ready this time. I pointed to the Allens' driveway, told him to skirt the oak tree as close as possible, then angle back across County Road 50. Still, as he backed up to the garage, the driver began shaking his head.

"That phone line's too low!" he called out. "I'll snag it on the way out!"

The power lines were on the Allens' side of the road. But the telephone lines ran along our side—high enough across the mouth of the driveway for both the moving van and dump truck to pass beneath. But not high enough if you raised the bed of the dump truck on the way out. Which is how the driver intended to spread his load, raising the bed while driving from the garage straight into the road. Spilling gravel behind him.

. . . *sunnuvabitch wires!*

I was livid. Because the only solution was to dump the entire load in the parking area to the left, which created a mountain of gravel higher than the garage door itself. I'd ordered enough 18 millimeter gravel to refurbish the driveway four inches deep, gravel I'd now have to spread by hand in the days to come, shoveling it into the wheelbarrow, trundling it around, scattering it about, and raking it smooth—covering 2,500 square feet from the road to the garage door. Which killed the rest of my free time after summer school and forced me to put off painting the house until the following year.

Elaine brought out Gatorade in sympathy.

"Do you realize," I said to her, pointing back and forth between the pitcher's mound and the black swath in the ditch, then from the weed-laced driveway to the mountain of gravel, "it's all because that woman didn't want ditches!"

I was hot, tired, and disgusted, having just overloaded the wheelbarrow with gravel—which rendered it tippy—dumping its load halfway to my target.

Elaine fell silent for a moment, then smiled. "If a man's home is his castle," she said finally, "then his ditch is his moat. Ever think of it that way?"

No, I hadn't.

Not even remotely.

. . .

As soon as that mountain of gravel had slid from the dump truck, I realized I'd ordered the wrong size. It was smaller than what we already had. But there was nothing to do short of shoveling it all back into the truck.

And as soon as I finished spreading it, of course, the cats next door discovered it. I found their dainty turds daily on my way to hunt for the morning paper. So I drove back to Furrows for something called Ro-pel (or was it Ro-don't?), an animal repellent that smelled worse than our ditch after the leech field drained through it.

The label on the plastic squirt bottle had small Disneylike pictures of what the product repelled—armadillos, badgers, birds, chipmunks, deer, gophers, moles, mice, prairie dogs, rabbits, raccoons, rats, and . . .

cats! "This unique blend of ingredients," the label said, "causes a mild irritation to animals' nasal passages, triggering the natural instinct to escape or avoid."

The ingredients included dried blood, putrescent whole egg solids, garlic oil, acetic acid, potassium salt, cloves, fish oil, onions, meat meal, seaweed, vitamin E, and wintergreen. Those last two seemed out of place, but there was only one thing to be said for the entire concoction—*peeYEW!*

It certainly got the job done. And then, quite unexpectedly, our neighbors to the west moved out, taking their cats with them. So I stored the Ro-pel (or was it Ro-don't?) in the pool shed, hoping the chemicals in there would lessen its stink. Which is when I began to think about those rusty mousetraps.

As with the flyswatters in the Florida room, I suddenly realized why there were mousetraps in the pool shed. Where there are fields, there are field mice. And where there are cats, the field mice have a natural enemy. But the cats had just moved out. Which meant that the mice, with the coming cool weather of autumn, would move in. Unmolested.

Which is exactly what happened.

So I drove back to Furrows, bought half a dozen brand new mousetraps, baited them with bits of cheese, and set them in the pool shed and Florida room. That night I left the sliding glass door open between the master bedroom and the Florida room so I could listen through the screen. Sure enough, those mousetraps went off like a string of firecrackers—*Snap! Snap! Snap!*—and in the morning, after the school bus had left, I took six dead mice by the tail and tossed them into my burning pen, their little bodies stiff with *rigor mouse-sis.*

I thought then that we had the situation well under control. But one evening a few weeks later, while we were gathered in the family room watching *Jeopardy!*, Elaine happened to look up and see something gray streaking between the dishwasher and refrigerator.

"What was that?" she said to me later. She didn't want to give Owen and Adrian another reason to call the SPCA.

"There's only one way to find out."

After the boys were in bed, I set several mousetraps behind the refrigerator. They went *snap!* in the night. And in the morning, after the school bus had left, I tossed several more dead mice by the tail into my burning pen.

Elaine was amazed. "How many can there be?"

"It's an invasion," I said. "Did you see the counter by the toaster?" It was dotted with what looked like those chocolate sprinkles you put on ice cream. Only they weren't chocolate sprinkles. They were mouse turds. Exchanged by the mice for crumbs of toast.

"Goddam . . . mice!"

After the boys went to bed, I set several mousetraps beside the toaster. And by morning those mice were toast.

Yard Wars of the Ohio Outback

The Wind in the Willows

The stupidest thing I ever did on County Road 50 was plant twin willow trees on either side of the mouth of the driveway. I wanted shade out front, and someone said that willows grew quickly—three feet per year. Which is an understatement if there ever was one.

So I bought two willow slips, stuck them in the ground to either side of the mouth of the driveway, and they grew like mutant Ninja turtles. Still, they were essential to my self-concept as a country squire. If I couldn't have a row of oaks shading my driveway like Tara in *Gone With the Wind*—oaks like the Allens' big one across the street took centuries to grow—I could have willows blowing in the wind. They'd certainly provide more shade than telephone poles laid end-to-end.

Planted as an afterthought after I'd regraveled the driveway, the willows would have to be battled for several years. Nonetheless, I was amazed at how quickly they grew. I swear, if you watch carefully, you can *see* a willow grow.

Meanwhile, I had two other trees to contend with, both apple. They were near the rear property line behind the boys' bedrooms, just to the left of the pool, halfway between the bluebird house and my burning pen. I had never owned apple trees before, so I didn't know what to expect. But what we came to expect were—well—apples. Thousands and thousands of apples. The previous owner had told me all about those apple trees before we moved in, but, as with the dishlike depression in the front yard, I was too excited to pay proper attention.

"This one's a Golden Delicious," she'd said, pointing to the tree on the left. I forget the name of the other. But after one taste of its red apples during our first fall on County Road 50, I christened it Goddam Delicious and ran into the house, insisting that Elaine and Owen and Adrian come right out, pick an apple from that tree, and take a bite. Which they did. And they agreed. Those apples were goddam delicious.

The problem with those apple trees was that they produced too many apples. And I never did a thing to encourage them. I think that planting a Golden Delicious next to a Goddam Delicious was supposed to entice them to have sex. To cross-pollinate with the bees or something. And it worked. But when the wind blew in the fall—the same wind that would eventually blow through the mutant willows flanking the driveway—it simply knocked all those golden apples and red apples to the ground. Which made walking around out there like walking on softballs.

The deer loved those apples. We'd watch them from the boys' bedroom windows in the fall. But they didn't eat enough to suit me. Other creatures came and went in the night, leaving little tooth marks on the fallen apples, or taking little bites—just small enough that you wouldn't bite into those apples yourself. Who wants to eat something a possum's been nibbling on? Or a raccoon or skunk? Of all the apples that fell, of course, these nocturnal creatures nibbled only the best ones, the perfectly round yellow ones and red ones, leaving the gnarled ones—like those apples from the orchards in Sherwood Anderson's *Winesburg, Ohio*—for Elaine's apple pies.

The apple battles began each autumn after the first windy day, when, upon returning from campus in the late afternoon, I'd have to go out back and toss the fallen apples into the cornfield. If I didn't, they'd turn to mush. Which, unlike walking on softballs, was like walking in applesauce spiced with buzzing bees. Owen and Adrian were no help—their arms would tire after they'd thrown but half a dozen each. And Elaine didn't get home from the Lima Library until after dark.

One day, amazed by the volume of apples that lay on the ground, I began to count them out of curiosity as I tossed them into the cornfield. I counted fifty or more, the next day sixty. On another afternoon, when there was no wind, I gave the Golden Delicious a good shaking—its branches were interlocked with the Goddam Delicious, making the two trees, in effect, one big goddam apple-producing machine—and apples bombarded me left and right, striking me on the head, shoulders, and back as I ducked for cover. Tossing them into the cornfield, I counted more than 200.

Together, those trees produced enough apples for every Adam and Eve in all the Bibles in existence, even though I left them to the mercy of the elements. I never once sprayed them. One year, after pruning them severely, hoping to curb their abundance, they produced twice as many apples as the year before. Several years later, when I pruned them again, they produced hardly a dozen, a state of affairs that would have puzzled Johnny Appleseed himself.

Ol' Johnny, who introduced the apple to large parts of Ohio, once raced thirty miles through the state from Mansfield to Mount Vernon to warn of impending Indian massacres and muster reinforcements. Had the settlers run out of ammunition, they could have shaken our trees—depending on the year and collective whim of the Golden and Goddam Delicious—and bombarded those Indians with apples.

. . .

Within a very few years those twin willows out front were shaking hands across the mouth of the driveway, overhanging the telephone lines, and littering the ditches with their long skinny leaves.

Entering the driveway was like going through a carwash, the kind with those dangling straps that swish back and forth as you drive on through. The long skinny branches of the willows hung right down to the ground, sweeping the gravel like a hula skirt and getting tangled in the Lawn Boy whenever I mowed the grass. They'd brush my back as I ducked beneath them. And when the wind was stiff, they'd flail me like a cat-o'-nine-tails.

They also blocked our vision as we left the driveway. This wasn't as much of a problem for Elaine, because she always turned the Merry Monza around when she left the garage in order to exit the driveway head first. Whereas I backed the Nova the length of the driveway right out into County Road 50.

I didn't realize how dangerous this was until a car zipped by me one day (the speed limit on County Road 50 was fifty-five miles per hour, but through traffic went faster), a car I hadn't even seen, although I'd looked both ways. Half a mile to our west was a slight dip in the road, and if a car happened to be in the dip when you looked in that direction, you wouldn't see it. So you'd look the other way, feel safe, and back into the road. At which point the car from the west would be about to plow into you broadside.

The second time this happened I knew I had to give those willows a haircut. One more strike, I figured, and I'd be out for good.

My initial hairstyle for those willows was a pageboy. I bobbed them straight across about waist high (my waist, that is) so I could get beneath them with the Lawn Boy and see clearly to the east and west before backing into the road. These haircuts were fun at first, because of the aesthetic aspect involved. I used an old manual hedge clipper, one I'd used on the long hedge across the front of the house before getting an electric trimmer. But then, like maintaining the pool, the maintenance became a pain in the ass.

I couldn't get the length even. Given the slight contour of the yard, I had to trim the willows' bangs at an angle, and when I'd walk up the street to see how I was doing, they'd look all out of whack. So I'd return to the trees with my manual hedge clipper and trim them some more. Then I'd walk up the street in the other direction, from where they'd look even more out of whack. By the time I was done trimming, those willows were sporting chest-high pageboys (my chest, that is.)

With all that trimming, of course, those willows—like the apple trees out back—only grew all the faster. So I countered with what I called the sno-cone, trimming them head high (my head, that is), so they looked like sno-cones. When that didn't work, I gave them a butch cut, sticking my extension ladder into the thick of their intertwining thicket of leaves and taking my electric chain saw to each gnarly branch above the main trunk. Which I lopped off and dragged across the harvested cornfield to dump in the distant woodlot—another remnant of the Great Black Swamp—where those branches eventually rotted.

But those lopped branches grew right back. Finally, before the main trunks of those willows could get any wider than the blade of my chainsaw, I cut them off at ground level, dragged them across the harvested cornfield, and dumped them in the swampy woodlot. Where they eventually rotted.

Not so the stumps that still flanked the driveway. To get rid of those—lest the willows rise from the dead—I bought a hand augur at Furrows with a one-inch-thick bit to drill holes in which to pour a special compound that was supposed to rot them from within. But those ironlike trunks snagged the augur, snapping it in two as I tried to wrestle it out.

. . . sunnuvabitch bit!

So I poured the compound all over each stump and waited. But it did no good either. Then I dug holes around those stumps and flailed away at them with the axe I'd bought after the ice storm in southwest Virginia. Wearing my ski goggles to protect my eyes from the flying chips, little by little I hacked them to pieces a few inches below ground level. Then I poured kerosene on them and set them ablaze, creating two smudge pots that burned for days. After which I filled in the holes with dirt from the cornfield and planted grass to conceal the graves.

This put an end to those willows. But not the wind that blew through them.

. . .

The severe wind from the Rocky Mountains that whips across the Great Plains gets to the east coast by crossing western Ohio. Where, given the flatness of the land, there is nothing to stop it—except the covers of aboveground pools.

Another victim of that wind on County Road 50 was the brand-new basketball hoop I put up for Owen and Adrian in the parking area of our driveway. We'd left their old wooden backboard screwed to the peak above the garage on Christopher Circle, splurging on a new white fiberglass beauty, with an orange rim and white net, which I fixed to a black metal pole that extended like a telescope to any height you wanted. The boys insisted on the official ten feet—Adrian was big enough now to get the ball to the rim—so the official ten feet it was.

I dug the hole for that black metal pole with my trusty posthole digger and sunk that sucker firmly in cement. Then, for good measure, I filled it with gravel—the pole was hollow from top to bottom—to give it added ballast against the wind. In retrospect, I should have planted that backboard parallel to the garage door instead of perpendicular, which left it facing due west. So one morning a few years later, after an exceptionally windy night, we found the backboard lying on the ground. Weakened by the constant buffeting of the wind, the five-inch-wide metal pole had fatigued, cracked, and snapped in half.

The large white pine opposite the picture window met a similar fate. Again due to the wind. And my own stupidity.

Between that pine and the pitcher's mound was an ugly cluster of junk bushes with a thorny locust right in the middle. I kept this eyesore in check by trimming it straight up on all sides, until it formed, in effect, a dense rectangular column. One Memorial Day, having inherited an American flag that had draped the casket of a relative buried in Arlington National Cemetery, I got the idea of hanging that flag from a rope strung horizontally between the top of the white pine and the top of the thorny locust. Which I did, snatching a length of clothesline from Elaine's laundry area in the basement.

For several years in a row, on Memorial Day and the Fourth of July I'd drape that flag on that length of clothesline. It was an enormous flag, measuring ten feet by six, and it undulated softly, hung edgewise as it was to the prevailing west wind. My mistake was to leave that clothesline tied to the white pine, letting it hang down the trunk vertically, rather than restringing it each year. Had I left it tied to the locust—which was as hard as the willow stumps—nothing would have happened. But in time, as the white pine grew taller and taller, that rope slowly strangled it, tightening around its soft bark like a hangman's noose. Until one windy night it snapped in half like the basketball pole.

Of course, given what it could do to trees and basketball poles, that Rocky Mountain wind wreaked havoc with the leaves each fall, especially the brown brittle leaves on the Allens' big oak across the street. The size of dinner plates, those leaves often wound up in our ditch. But it wasn't the prevailing west wind that put them there. It was the sneaky northeast wind, the kind of weather event that turns the tables on meteorologists.

The fierce westerly winds simply sent the Allens' leaves sailing toward town. But a northeast wind sent them our way, filling the ditches knee-deep and scattering them across our entire acre. We had enough leaves of our own to deal with, what with two apple trees, two large swamp maples, two willows (while they lasted), and a rapidly growing row of swamp maples. But those swamp maples were just sticks in the ground the first time a nor'easter filled our ditch with those big brown dinner plates.

Which meant I had to rake them out of the ditch and into the yard, load them into the wheelbarrow, cart them back to the harvested cornfield, and scatter them among the stubble. This was always worse when it rained. Because I had to put on my boots, splash through ankle-deep water, and wrestle those soggy leaves into heavy wet piles. But if I didn't rake the leaves out of the ditches, the first good frost would make them heavier, they'd clog the wide pipe connecting the ditches beneath the mouth of the driveway, and the first good freeze would fix them in place. Then I'd have to break through an inch of ice in order to clean them out.

I expected none of this, of course, during our first fall on County Road 50, which was an idyllic Indian summer, as I recall. Then one night the wind shifted, and in the morning our ditch was filled with leaves from the Allens' big oak. I was livid.

. . . *sunnuvabitch wind!*

But that evening the westerly Rocky Mountain wind became my friend. We'd just switched to Daylight Savings Time, the boys were inside watching cartoons, and Elaine was on her way home from the Lima Library in the Merry Monza—when, under cover of early darkness, and with the help of a ferocious wind that made it difficult to stand upright, I ducked into the ditch like a thief, rake in hand, and began to sweep those big brown leaves into the road. The Rocky Mountain wind did the rest, whirling them skyward toward campus whence I'd just come, right past Christopher Circle.

Elaine swung into the driveway just as I was finishing, catching me in the full glare of the Merry Monza's headlights. With a merry grin on my face.

. . .

But that was the only favor ever granted me by the Rocky Mountain wind. Otherwise, it was a constant enemy, in large ways and small.

One of the latter involved the white pine out front, which considered itself a deciduous tree, shedding its needles each fall as if jealous of the swamp maples and the Allens' oak. This would begin at the end of October—just in time for Halloween—when the needles on that tree turned bright orange. They'd drop slowly at first, then by the thousands, creating an attractive orange ring around the base of the tree. But the slightest wind would shower them everywhere. A good blast of the Rocky Mountain wind would carry them all the way to the driveway, where raking them out of the gravel was as difficult as raking the lawn free of cottonwood fluff on Christopher Circle.

The wind knocked pinecones from the white pine as well. The taller that tree got—as it recovered from its beheading—the larger the pinecones grew and the farther they flew, sometimes ending up along our property line to the east. From where I'd kick them into our neighbor's yard, so when the divorcée came out to pick them up, she'd notice the grass her teenage son blew into *our* yard with their riding mower.

Scattered by the Rocky Mountain wind, those pinecones looked like white-tipped dog turds, the white tips courtesy of pine pitch, which made picking them up a pain in the ass. If you didn't wear gloves, the sticky pitch would glue your fingers together by the time you were done. If you *did* wear gloves, the sticky pitch would ruin them. I kept a five-gallon bucket in the garage for this annual fall chore, filling it daily for several weeks in a row and dumping it into my burning pen out back. After which, only kerosene would rid my hands of that pine pitch.

One afternoon Elaine commandeered my bucket of pinecones for an artsy-craftsy Martha Stewart kind of project. She intended to fashion a wreath for the front door from pinecones and coat hangers. I figured the pine pitch would scuttle that project, but I was wrong. She abandoned it when a large black beetle crawled out of one of the pinecones. After which I loaned her kerosene to get the sticky pitch off her fingers.

Pummeling the white pine in other seasons, the wind would scatter little green pickles about the size of your pinky finger—immature pinecones that hid in the grass until you stepped on them while mowing, an annoyance that led to an ambush I called "the bough in the brow." Which was actually due to a variety of factors.

When we first moved to County Road 50, the radius of the branches extending from the bottom of the white pine was about ten feet, a length that doubled in the ensuing years. Nearest the trunk, these branches fattened to a diameter of five inches, and due to the force of gravity they dipped at the end, making it difficult to mow beneath them. So it was only natural to trim them. Which I did with my short bow saw, leaving its blade—and my fingers—sticky with pine pitch.

Every few years I'd lop off the ends of the branches to get them to rise a bit in order to maintain enough space to pass beneath with the Lawn Boy. Still, I had to crouch and duck my head when passing beneath, which I always did at top speed, since it took me two and a half hours to mow the entire acre.

The first of many times I caught a bough in the brow—whacking my head on the bottom branch—I was wearing a straw hat to protect my face from the sun. It protected my face, all right, but it also blocked my view. And when I stepped on one of those little green pickles, I lost my focus, looked up, and whacked my head.

"Goddam . . . pine!"

I should have cut it down then and there. But its trunk was already wider than the blade of my chainsaw.

Ohio Interstate Takeoff

I left on a Monday—the whole of America ahead of me—toward the end of a summer filled with disasters both natural and man-made. The East Coast was burning up, the West Coast was burning down, and the hurricane season was brewing in the Atlantic like a manic coffeepot. We had endured the loss of John-John and a string of mass murders and were in the throes of the Y2K countdown. Hurricane Dennis had lingered through Labor Day, confounding the economy along the Eastern Seaboard, ending vacations prematurely, and sending children back to school in a sour mood. But in Ohio all was green and quiet. Our little village of Ada had somehow escaped the droughts that were ravaging the nation. The weather had been beautiful for days—blue skies and low humidity with temperatures no more than eighty—absolutely perfect for my departure. Until the very last minute.

Sunday night I woke to what sounded like rain on the roof. Then my big day dawned dark and drizzly, foggy and cold—Charles Lindbergh weather. An Internet check revealed that Hurricane Floyd was on the way, a Category 4 storm threatening to become a "Cat-5." Weather-watchers were unanimous in their warnings: "Keep a very, very close eye on the progress of this major hurricane!" But there was more. The season's ninth tropical depression had been upgraded to a tropical storm—Gert. I'd have to deal with both her and her big brother a week or so down the road. "No teeth for the present," I mused stoically, as Macbeth had said of Banquo's son.

Backing the 'Vette from the garage at 8:15, I hit a switch and the headlights somersaulted out of the sleek hood to reveal the slanting rain. It was the first time I had used the headlights, the first time the car had ever been rained on. Not good vibes. In the headlights' full glare my wife and older son, who had not yet returned to college (our younger son was already on campus, beginning his freshman year), stood silhouetted in the garage like criminals, their shadows large on the wall. But there was only one criminal in our rural neighborhood that morning—*me*. I was abandoning home, job, and family (with everyone's blessing!) to pursue a long-standing personal dream. With a toot of the horn I slipped into the fog like a thief, then headed up Main Street to I-75, passing a colleague on her way in to work. She glanced at the 'Vette but didn't see me, the day dark enough without my tinted windows. I could imagine the classes she'd be teaching, the meetings she'd attend, and suddenly I was buoyant, gripped by a giddy sense of release. The brief encounter helped me focus on the task ahead. This woman's husband had argued that interstate medians should be used for rail service, and as I reached the entrance ramp it seemed like an idea worth exploring.

I-75 to Toledo cuts through the wide-open outback of northwest Ohio. The terrain—mostly farmland planted with corn, wheat, and soybeans—is flat, but not oppressively so. In some places it might be said to roll, but I have a friend in Maryland who says I'm deceived by this, that I've been living in Ohio for too long. Still, the I–75 landscape has two distinct features I would see nowhere else in America. The first is an abundance of farm ponds. You see a farm pond every few minutes. At every entrance, exit, and overpass farm ponds hug the highway to either side. Some are fringed with cattails, others have sandy beaches, and a few are protected from the west wind by rows of white pine. The shorelines are ringed with riprap, chunky gray quarry stone that prevents the banks from eroding. Almost all are rectangular—some long and thin, others nearly square—but very few are round, the more natural shape you'd expect.

Why all the ponds? The answer is simple. When I-75 was constructed in the late fifties and early sixties, fill dirt was needed for access ramps and inclines. Rather than truck the dirt in, engineers dug it on the spot. The result was a host of "borrow pits," precise excavations several acres in size. Then nature took over. Rain and run-off turned the pits into farm ponds, and state officials worked with local farmers to stock them. If the farmers didn't want fish, the birds stocked them anyway. Migrating ducks and geese and other waterfowl encounter a good deal of fish eggs. When they take off, the fish go with them, populating the next pond down the road. At least that's what the biologists tell me.

The second feature—totally annoying compared to the pastoral farm ponds—is the woodlots. Having grown up back East, I'm used to forests that run on and on. You can't tell where they begin and you can't tell where they end. Eastern forests are continuous, but not so in northwest Ohio, where "forest" is entirely the wrong word. Trees occur across the horizon in scattered woodlots ranging in size from a few acres to several hundred. Ohio was once totally forested, but pioneers developed special methods of clear-cutting, notching trunks across a wide area so that the crash of a single tree would tumble many more like matchsticks. Once the land was cleared and the stumps had been exhumed, subsequent growths returned—where allowed—in neurotic units. Hence the regular blocks of elm, oak, swamp maple, thorny locust, and tall cottonwoods that fill the air in summer with a pillowy fluff.

A landscape of woodlots takes some getting used to. Treed stretches end as abruptly as they begin—end and begin, end and begin. The discontinuity is irritating, offending some sensibility deep within the self in the way that small children are disturbed by disembodied figures. And the woodlots cause a more practical problem: they bring the deer out of hiding, in search of vegetation at the very next woodlot. In the early morning you can see the deer bounding from block to block, leaping above the corn, wheat, and soybeans. I used to mistake them for large dogs, but they're faster and more nimble. The Ohio Division of Wildlife estimates that there are half a million deer in the state right now. Everybody knows someone who's hit one with a car, if they haven't hit one themselves. Diamond-shaped yellow signs with the silhouette of a leaping buck warn you where they cross I-75.

But not this morning. In the rain and fog and spray of mist from the trucks I couldn't see those yellow signs, let alone the farm ponds and woodlots. Traffic was heavier than I had expected—as many trucks as cars—and construction areas demanded careful attention. Thanks to President Clinton's record $203 billion highway bill, summer motorists had been warned to expect construction about every forty miles. It was still summer, and the predictions proved correct. I encountered two such areas before I had gone fifty miles.

At 9:30 I pulled into a rest area just south of Bowling Green. The outside temperature, according to my dashboard monitor, had risen to a damp sixty-five degrees. I-75 rest areas are welcome oases—entirely green, entirely clean. This one was no exception. Trucks to the left, cars to the right. Then an attractive brick comfort station, with picnic tables and charcoal grills along winding sidewalks though a grove of tall trees. I parked among a host of empty spaces at the far end of the lot, just beyond a green Corvette the same year as mine. Its driver, returning from the brick building, waved briefly, and the unexpected gesture thrilled me, my first ever from a fellow 'Vette owner, confirming my membership in some sort of club. In the weeks to come I would count fifty-eight Corvettes around the nation—mostly in Texas and Florida—exchanging salutes with many of the drivers. But that initial nod of recognition seemed to validate my mission, a moment of Corvette karma that dispelled the uncertainty I was beginning to feel about getting out of my own 'Vette to ask total strangers about the interstates.

I had begun my interviews at home, surprised by my wife's negative response. But the fault was my own. In my enthusiasm for the interstates, I had completely forgotten Elaine's interstate traumas. But they were twenty years ago!

"How could you forget?" she said in disbelief. "I was pregnant with Owen when I hit that icy bridge on I-270."

We were living in Rockville, Maryland, at the time, and she was on her way to work. It had begun to snow. The long curving bridge that connects I-270 to the I-495 D.C. beltway had glazed over, and its toothlike expansion joints sent our old Impala into a spin. The car struck the left abutment while a tractor trailer slipped by on the right, then hit the right abutment as another trailer passed on the left. Elaine escaped with a concussion, Owen safe in her womb, but the Impala was demolished.

"And then there was that guy on I-81," she continued. "Remember? Right after we moved to Virginia? I was going up to Roanoke in the Monza. Owen was strapped into his car seat beside me, when that creep in a Jeeplike vehicle pulled alongside."

The creep was masturbating, keeping pace with the Monza so Elaine couldn't miss the show. It did nothing for her appreciation of interstate highways.

I turned to Owen for help. "You were along for the ride on both those occasions," I said. "What do *you* think?"

"Of the interstates?"

"Yes."

"Well—" Owen thought for a moment. "I guess my stance is more philosophical than Mom's." He'd been commuting 200 miles round trip down I-75 to an internship in Dayton. "I see the Interstates as the Great In-Between. I'm sort of mystified by the contrast between their impersonal nature and the aesthetic appeal of the symmetry of moving vehicles."

I turned to Elaine, who laughed and shook her head. "Men!"

"Why don't you ask Adrian?" Owen suggested.

So I asked his brother, Adrian, who had just got his driver's license. "For me," he said, "the interstates are simply fast and exciting. They turn a routine run up I-75 to the Findlay Mall into a big adventure."

In contrast to my family, one of my colleagues dismissed my query outright. "The trucks have ruined the interstates," he barked. "You'll see!"

Out of the rain in the brick building, I approached an attractive young woman by the water fountain. "The interstates?" she said. "I don't know. I slept most of the way. *He* drove." She nodded at her husband, who was exiting the men's room, staring at me as if I was trying to pick up his wife. Remembering my own wife's trauma, I suddenly became self-conscious. The last thing I wanted was to become an interstate intimidator.

"We drove all night from Florida," the husband said bluntly, reclaiming his wife by putting an arm around her shoulder. "We're heading home to Michigan. The interstates are less crowded at night because the trucks pull off to sleep. There are no towns, no stops, so it's an easy roll. A straight shot home. Ready, honey?" He turned his back on me and they walked away.

An elderly Canadian gentleman, waiting for his wife, was less threatened by me. "The interstates are the only roads we ever take for any distance," he said. "They're clean, well serviced, and in good shape. We're just returning from Branson, Missouri."

Outside again—the rain had let up—I explained to a lanky trucker and his shorter driving partner what my colleague had said about trucks ruining the interstates.

"You tell that guy," the tall one said, "that everything in his home is delivered by trucks. The railroads can't do it as fast. The economy would fold without trucks on the interstates."

His partner tugged on the bill of his cap, anxious to get back on the road. "The main problem for us is the damn construction. It's dangerous 'cause it takes so long to get done. They's always draggin' their feet. Meanwhile, people's gettin' killed."

On my way back to the 'Vette I took note of two signs. One said *Welcome to Ohio . . . The Heart of It All,* a message repeated in German, Spanish, Japanese, French, and Italian—the only interstate sign I would see in all of America in more than two languages. The second, which I'd see more frequently, said *The Dwight D. Eisenhower System of Interstate Highways,* its words surrounded by five white stars for the five-star general. Having never served in the military, I gave it my best Corvette salute.

It started raining again—hard—as I continued north to Toledo, where I picked up I-80 and my grand lap officially began. Until then I had felt like Sal Paradise in Jack Kerouac's *On the Road:* "All the way up I'd been worried about the fact that on this, my big opening day, I was only moving north." It was the late forties and Sal was headed west. But I was heading east. Why? Why not lap America counterclockwise? Except for a few hundred miles between Albany and Boston and again between Orono, Maine, and the Canadian border, I was familiar with the interstates on the first leg of my journey as far as Savannah, Georgia. By heading east I was saving the best for last. Beyond Savannah—if anything was left down there after Floyd and Gert had done their dirt—the thousands of miles remaining would be new for me all the way around to Chicago, just five hours from home.

Stopping for a ticket at the tollbooth, I was overwhelmed by a sense of occasion. I imagined myself in one of those toy Hot Wheels Corvettes on a huge relief map of America—large enough to cover an entire basketball court—with its raised mountain ranges, color-coded elevations, and long blue rivers. My little car was pointing east from Toledo and I had ten thousand miles ahead of me, the entire circumference of the forty-eight states. As I plucked the ticket from the automatic metal mouth, I was struck by the enormity of what I was undertaking. Then the ticket was in my shirt pocket and I flew from the gate.

I-80—the Ohio Turnpike—is a toll road that doubles as I-90 until Cleveland. It was undergoing major construction. A third lane was being added, service plazas were being renovated, and interchanges were being renumbered to conform to Federal Highway Administration standards. The most disturbing result of these improvements was the absence of a median strip. The shallow V-shaped grassy divider I had taken for granted on I-75 had been sacrificed for extra lanes, paved over and replaced by a low concrete wall. This put the opposing traffic at what seemed like arm's length, and with nothing but mudguards and mist surrounding me for miles, I sought relief shortly before noon at the Commodore Perry Travel Center.

I was glad I stopped. The place was brand new. The former service plaza, with room for dozens of trucks and hundreds of cars, had shut you in like a prisoner, its sprawling ugly buildings devoid of windows. The new facility looks like a community college, its main redbrick building centered about a bright rotundalike dome that opens to the sky like an observation deck. Three portecocheres extend from the dome toward ample parking areas, each offering a separate entrance, skylights, and protection from the weather. Inside, the smoke-free environment requires proper dress, and the concept of a travel center is more than a euphemism. There are sparkling restrooms, telephones, a business area, ATM machines, copy machines, Internet access, postal services, a game room, a vending area, and an information desk. But the main attraction is the domed food court, with all the glassy high-ceilinged ambience of a swanky mall in a modern airport terminal. Businesses include Starbucks Coffee, Burger King, Jodi Maroni's (home of the *haut dog*), Cinnabon, Sbarro's, and Max & Irma's. Tables and chairs extend outside for patio dining. Gasoline pumps and service bays, equally open and accessible, lie beyond. Farthest off is the pet "exercise area," and there's even a kennel. New trees and shrubs had been planted, but the grass seed had not yet germinated. Above the main entrance stood a tall white concrete sculpture—three narrow obelisks each taller than the next—like X-Acto knives or the tail fins of jets. I couldn't quite figure it out. It seemed to reflect the Wright Brothers more than Commodore Perry, local hero of the War of 1812. Still, any effort at placing art in public places must be applauded. Inside, I stopped to inquire about the sculpture, but the information desk was unattended. Drop me a note if you know what that thing is.

By the time I returned to the 'Vette the rain had stopped, the sun was threatening to break through, and the temperature had risen to seventy. A flock of seagulls was scavenging in the freshly paved parking lot, an incongruous presence. But Lake Erie, never seen from I-80, is just a few miles north.

At one o'clock I paid a $2.95 toll and left I-80 on I-90 for Cleveland. In clear weather you can glimpse Cleveland from twenty miles out—a nondescript brown skyline—but today's overcast made it impossible. Like many Rust Belt cities, Cleveland comes at you with a bleak median divider, dirty brick factories, smokestacks, cranes, and rows and rows of Archie Bunker houses. Then a high bridge over the Cuyahoga River gorge dumps you downtown in a maze of viaducts and overpasses. Buildings fly by—a tall structure like New York's Chrysler Building, a more attractive stair-step affair, and some glassy modern fronts that have not yet lost their shine. Below and left sit Jacobs Field and Gund Arena. But I had little time for rubbernecking. The road surface was horrendous—beat-up and bone-jarring—the worst I would see until New Orleans. The *Places Rated Almanac* had just named Cleveland the No. 2 recreation area in the nation, second only to (no surprise here) New Orleans. All those visitors must account for the battered roads, which local drivers seem to ignore. Meanwhile, my back was taking a severe pounding.

The Corvette, because it rides so low, is notorious for its rough ride, although late-model engineering has addressed that problem. My 'Vette had sports seats, which inflate in crucial places—at the base of the spine, midback, and between the shoulder blades. They also push up at the waist, as if you're being hugged by someone standing in front of you. Having twice had back surgery for a herniated disk,

the latest operation—according to plan—just six weeks before departure, I could never have driven a 'Vette without sports seats. But the
interstate through Cleveland put me in such pain I had visions of
having to abandon my grand lap on the very first day—like those
'round-the-world balloonists who abort their flight after lift-off due
to some colossal mechanical failure. Or error in judgment.

Ignoring the potholes and slick pavement, the midday traffic
whizzed by. A woman in a white car cut in front of me, gesticulating
wildly, cigarette in one hand, cell phone in the other. So who's driving? I wondered. It's impossible to signal with a cell phone in your
hand. That's one reason that death by cell phone has increased more
rapidly than death by road rage. The Cleveland suburb of Brooklyn
had recently passed a law prohibiting driving with handheld phones,
the first such legislation in the nation. Obviously this woman wasn't
from Brooklyn. I had a notion to send her the article about the new
law that I'd clipped from the paper, but she swerved—once again
without signaling—cutting off the guy on my right. Then she was
gone before I could get her license number.

Leaving Cleveland brings an interstate surprise. The road cuts
sharply to the right and suddenly Lake Erie's on your left not a hundred yards away—a wall of dark water all the way to the horizon,
a quivering meniscus on the beaker of Ohio. I thought of the little
Dutch boy with his finger in the dike. Remove that finger and I-90
would wash away! Then Lake Erie plays peek-a-boo with the trees
and waterfront homes—brimming along rock jetties, beaches, and
boats—before it disappears for good behind a long tan wall. That wall
runs for miles, ragged trees rising above its stucco surface. Built for
privacy, or as a sound barrier, or to block pollution and headlights,
it's the type of urban interstate wall I would see all too frequently.
This one varies in height from about six feet to sixteen. But the variety
does nothing for the aesthetics.

Fortunately, the pavement smoothed out beyond the Cleveland
city limits and I dismissed my back pain as opening day tension. At
two o'clock I stopped at a rest area to stretch and recover, in the process learning something about the interstates without having to ask.
A bespectacled teenager approached me, wanting to know if he was
on the road to Chagrin Falls. I took out my atlas, placed it on the roof

of the 'Vette, and opened it to Ohio. "You are *here*," I said, stabbing a finger at the page, "and you want to be *there*. You missed your turn. You have to go a little farther and turn around." He looked at me quizzically, disconcerted.

"I know all that," he said finally. "I have a map and directions in the car. I'm looking for someone I can follow to get back on route."

I tossed the atlas into the car. "Sorry," I said. "I need the men's room."

He was gone when I came out, but a second young man approached me, looking like a college freshman late for his first class. I know that look, because I teach a lot of freshmen that are late for their first class. Incredibly, he too was lost. He needed to turn around and go back to the Mentor exit.

"You just missed your ride," I said, explaining about the other guy to make him feel better.

The obvious lesson is that, for some people, the interstates can be totally disorienting. And ironically amusing. One traveler was chagrined. The other needed a mentor. And the latter wouldn't let me go, lapsing into a discourse about his laptop computer when he saw the vanity plates on the 'Vette—LAP USA. He wanted to know what kind of laptop I was using. *He* had an Apple Powerbook G3/300 with third-generation power PC chips and he was going to speed-bump that puppy to 400 megahertz. What did I think of *that?* I told him I thought Megahertz was a giant car-rental company and he shook his head in disgust.

Back on the highway I learned from National Public Radio that Gert was now officially the fifth hurricane of the season. But Floyd was coming first, with winds of 155 miles per hour. And just when it looked like the weather at least might clear up in Ohio, all vehicles streaming at me from Erie had their headlights on. It was raining to the east, the sky gray overhead but much darker in the distance. Good old dreary Erie, more than an hour away but already living up to its reputation. Some definite confluence of weather elements, moving west to east across America, funnels all bad weather through the Great Lakes to Erie. You can actually watch it happening from the interstate, where the meteorology is more reliable than on the six o'clock news.

Before we leave Ohio, here's an interstate item, from an article by Mark Williams of the Associated Press, regarding the completion of I-670 through downtown Columbus, the state capital:

Finishing the half-mile stretch will mark the end of nearly fifty years of construction of Ohio's Interstate System, and Clark Street, president of the Ohio Contractors Association and a former transportation executive, didn't think he'd live to see the day. As was the case across the nation, most of Ohio's 1,300 miles of Interstate were built in the nineteen fifties, sixties, and seventies. Interstate 670 was designed through Columbus with economic development in mind, to make it easier to reach the northwest side of town, a major growth area. The connector runs from Interstate 70 on the city's west side to Interstate 270 on the northeast side near Port Columbus International Airport. Planning for the final segment began in 1965, with construction to begin in 1976, but a variety of problems, from funding to environmental concerns, postponed the start until 1993. According to Street, completion of the Interstate System in Ohio is a tribute to the people who planned it, the contractors who built it, and the public who paid for it.

Street concluded with a fascinating thought: An entire generation of Americans has grown up thinking that the interstates have always existed.

Yard Wars of the Ohio Outback

Dog Daze

When our neighbors to the west moved out with their cats, new neighbors with dogs moved in.

At first there were just two dogs (and two kids as well, both younger than Owen and Adrian)—a dachshund I called Big Mama and a cocker spaniel I called Bark. But Big Mama soon gave birth to five little thoroughbred sausages that the neighbors intended to raise and sell. I called them, respectively, Yip, Yap, Yak, Yipe, and Yelp. Of course, the new neighbors immediately enclosed their backyard with a sturdy wire fence to contain these dogs. But they did nothing to contain their barking, which began whenever I stepped outside and continued until I went back in.

It drove me mad. Those dogs acted as if I were the intruder. They'd bark from dawn 'til dusk as long as I was out in the yard. The only time I couldn't hear them was when I mowed the lawn. They didn't care for the Lawn Boy, and it gave me great pleasure to roar down our property line between the pitcher's mound and the cornfield, with those dogs right on the other side of their wire fence—a-yippin', yappin', yakkin', yipin', and yelpin'. With an occasional bark from Bark and Big Mama.

Otherwise, Chip and Lynn were wonderful neighbors. Lynn stayed at home to look after the kids, and Chip was a university colleague, a new assistant professor in industrial technology—which is what, in junior high, we used to call "shop." But the wood shop and mechanical drawing of yesteryear had morphed into the CAD-CAM and robotics of today, and Chip was a master of all such things. With the help of his students, he patented an ingenious gismo that was actually launched into space. (A few years later, he would leave the university to work for NASA, taking wife and kids—and those seven dogs—with him.)

Chip's handiwork around the house put me to shame. He re-shingled his own roof, enlarged the garage, and poured himself a concrete driveway. Then, to alleviate water problems in the basement, he rented a backhoe, tiled his own drains, and engineered a run from the cornfield to the ditch. Next, he converted part of the garage into a workshop that contained every kind of tool imaginable—from drill presses to circular table saws—wherein he moonlighted as a refurbisher of furniture, including a player piano that rolled out of the moving van the day they rolled in.

Of course, I couldn't go over to chat with Chip without all those dogs a-yippin', yappin', yakkin', yipin', yelpin', and barkin' up a storm. So I rarely went over. But Chip was always there, like a good neighbor, when we needed him.

One morning, just at dawn, a vicious rainstorm ripped through Hardin County, splitting the main trunk of the swamp maple that hung over our master bedroom. A tremendous jolt on the roof sent me scrambling to the window, where my view was obscured by leaves and branches. An eerie silence followed. Then came the sound of a chainsaw. Chip was up in the swamp maple with a gasoline-powered chainsaw—its blade three times the length of mine—dicing that sucker into lengths of firewood.

That winter, after a blizzard buried northwest Ohio beneath four feet of snow, closing local schools for days, the first sound we heard in the silent chill of dawn was Chip's snowblower clearing our driveway after he'd cleared his own. The snow had drifted across the top of our garage door and filled the driveway to a similar depth all the way to the road.

I didn't have time to warn Chip about the gravel—the snowblower shot it all over the yard like a machine gun, forcing me to rake it up and pick it out of the grass by hand come spring. But hey, this was an emergency. We were out of milk and other staples, and we'd have starved had Chip not blasted us clear, freeing us from the blizzard so we could get into town once the plows cleared County Road 50 the following day.

Wising up to these winters in the country, I got a brilliant idea for a snow fence that I thought would keep our long gravel driveway free of snow forever. It was to be built from materials I already had in the basement—the large coil of wire fencing and metal stakes from the previous owner's dog pen and the leftover railings from our deck on Christopher Circle, which I'd salvaged along with the boys' play-fort when we moved.

I took the rails next door to Chip's workshop, and while the dogs were a-yippin', yappin', yakkin', yipin', yelpin', and barkin', he sliced them lengthwise with his circular table saw, leaving me with a pile of thin wooden slats each thirty-six inches long. These I took to my own garage and painted with white paint that I'd bought for the house trim. Then I lugged that big coil of wire fencing up from the basement and strung it parallel to the driveway, from the far end of the hedge to the edge of the ditch, just to the west of the white pine, effectively dividing the front yard in half.

My brilliant idea was to weave the white slats through that wire fence, producing the kind of slatted fence that protects sand dunes from the wind along the seashore. Instead, I produced what looked like one of the wattle stick fences you find in the remote villages of Russia. Unlike the thin pliable wire of seaside dune fences, the dog wire of my snow fence was simply too thick and rigid to allow for an easy interweaving of those wooden slats, many of which snapped when I bent them, forcing me to repair them with duct tape. Others bowed like my bow saw, sticking out from the fence at odd angles both top and bottom.

"It looks awful," Elaine said when I finished. "Owen and Adrian are embarrassed to get on the school bus."

"They'll appreciate it," I said, "when they don't have to shovel the driveway this winter."

But, of course, they *would* have to shovel the driveway that winter. Because the first good storm didn't come from the west. It was a sneaky nor'easter, leaving the yard between the snow fence and the pitcher's mound with a dusting of snow while filling the driveway to a depth of three feet.

"Goddam . . . fence!"

"You're a country squire," Elaine said. "Not a Russian peasant."

. . .

The following year, undaunted, I purchased a blaze-orange plastic snow fence twenty-five yards long and strung it where my wattle fence had been. And this started a craze. Several weeks later half a dozen neighbors along County Road 50 had plastic snow fences flanking their long driveways, all of them a conservative black plastic. But hey, somebody has to set the fashion trend. I was hoping the garish blaze-orange strip dividing our front yard would blind the memory of my wattle snow fence.

But that winter the snow fence proved useless. The weather was mild—I recall planting grass seed in the middle of February—so it was difficult to judge its potential efficacy. Not so the following winter, when the Rocky Mountain wind blasted us constantly, filling the driveway with snow because I'd strung the fence in the wrong place—it needed to be closer to the driveway, not at the far end of the hedge—and it was impossible to move because the ground had frozen. Time and again we had to shovel the snow the length of the driveway, piling it to each side. And time and again the whipping winds drifted it shut, until it seemed like snow was something that fell horizontally.

The winter after that—when I adjusted the position of the snow fence at the outset—was another mild one. And the year after that was a year of nor'easters, rendering the blaze-orange snow fence, in its new position, a blazing white elephant. It proved effective only one year in seven, so I eventually rolled it up and stuck it in the pool shed beside R2D2 Jr., long after my neighbors had given up on theirs.

But winter in northwest Ohio brought an enemy worse than snow—snowmobiles. The cowpokes that rode these suckers were reckless. You could hear their engines roaring in the surrounding fields long before you saw them. The stupidest ones sped right down the middle of County Road 50. After the area roads had been plowed-and-sanded and bare blacktop was showing, they'd resort to the ditches, sweeping in and out of them ever so briefly to cross the mouth of your driveway.

Which was exceedingly dangerous. After several days of shoveling we'd have a wall of snow six feet high down each side of the driveway—higher than Owen and Adrian and the roof of the Merry Monza. I piled it even higher at the ditches in order to discourage snowmobilers from cutting across the mouth of the driveway. But they'd just blast right through those snow walls as though breaching the Alamo. And keep on going. What if the Merry Monza had been parked there? Or if Owen and Adrian were playing in the driveway on their day off from school?

I raised such questions in a letter to the editor of the *Lima News*. After which, of course, as if in retaliation, the cowardly cowpokes returned on their snowmobiles under cover of darkness, their headlights climbing the venetian blinds in the master bedroom as they did donuts around the white pine out front before zooming off, carving tracks in the ground that were still visible come spring. My fantasy was to string a thin wire across the ditch at the mouth of the driveway and behead a few of the bastards, to protect the lives of my family. I got the idea when I read of a snowmobiler beheaded in such fashion by a barbed-wire fence. But Elaine brought me to my senses.

"If I put it low enough," I argued, "it'd catch the snowmobile itself and the rider would go flying."

"And break his neck on the telephone pole."

What I did instead was keep vigil and chase a few offenders in the Merry Monza. In theory, if you followed the snowmobile tracks far enough, you'd eventually catch the culprits. But they'd always cut into the cornfields to escape. For all my trouble I caught only one offender. And it didn't require much of an effort.

My citizen's arrest was based on a simple principle of physics: What goes into town on County Road 50, must come out of town on County Road 50. And so late one afternoon when a snowmobile roared across the mouth of our driveway, I went out front and concealed myself in the ditch, awaiting its return. Then I stood tall to flag down the sunnuvabitch. I was so mad I never gave much thought about what to do next.

It was a tense moment. I'd never encountered anyone in such a situation before. But I had a reputation to uphold as a published author of a letter in the *Lima News*. And sure enough, twenty minutes later—true to the law of snowmobile physics—I heard the roar of the returning snowmobile. Coming right at me at top speed.

"Halt!" I yelled, jumping up and waving my arms like a football ref signaling time-out. Incredibly, the snowmobile skidded to a halt. Then the driver, in full snowmobile garb, dismounted and stood up. He looked like an astronaut, with a Darth Vader–like helmet obscuring his face.

"Take off your hat!" I ordered. And he took off his hat.

"Hello, sir," the driver said sheepishly. It was Dallas Hoffman, one of Adrian's classmates. A polite kid who played guitar in the high school swing band.

Goddam sunnuvabitch Dallas!

Disgusted, I turned my back, stepped from the ditch, and stomped back inside.

. . .

But the worst winter we ever experienced on County Road 50 was the year of the ice storm, which wreaked havoc on northwest Ohio more than a decade after I arrested Dallas in the ditch. The iceman that cameth that year putteth to shame the ice storm we'd survived in southwest Virginia. Chip and Lynn had moved out by then. Owen and Adrian, too.

It began with torrential rains on a Wednesday afternoon in January, followed by freezing temperatures that night. I first noticed something was wrong right after supper when I heard a growling noise outside the family room window, beneath which sat our heat pump. Its giant fan blades, laced with ice from a northeast wind, were wobbling, causing the entire unit to shake, putting it in danger of wobbling right off its cement base.

I solved the problem with the glass door from the boys' shower stall that Jim Massillo had replaced years earlier. I'd stored the old door in the basement, thinking it might come in handy for I-don't-know-what. But now I knew exactly what it could be used for. I leaned it at an angle against the face of the heat pump, blocking its huge fan blades from the rain and wind. And as soon as the unit stopped wobbling, I went back inside, totally satisfied with myself for having bested the elements.

But by morning, of course, driven by that tricky nor'easter, which had intensified during the night, every tree, phone line, and power line in northwest Ohio had snapped under the weight of a ton of ice. Unlike the ice storm in Virginia, it wasn't pretty. No sun rose to proclaim a glistening fairyland. Skies remained gray, the wind nasty, the scene in all directions apocalyptic. Out front our white pine looked maimed. It had lost every bough on its north side, as if hacked by a giant machete. The swamp maples, too, had lost limbs.

The shotgun-like sound of cracking trees that had kept us awake all night continued well into the morning. Local schools closing for the day soon closed for the week, once the enormity of the destruction became evident. The university closed, too—for the first time in its history—when water froze in the dorm toilets.

Local officials declared a state of emergency in all neighboring counties. No vehicles were allowed on the highways except for police cars and ambulances—you'd be arrested on sight. The streets were impassable, anyway. A university colleague, braving County Road 50 in defiance of the law, had to swerve to avoid an enormous limb that dropped like a bomb from the Allens' oak, sending him flying right into the Allens' ditch.

I put on my ski togs and ran out to help. But our driveway was a sheet of ice, and because of the contour of our property, I nearly skated right down it into County Road 50. We could have used those telephone poles now, but they were at Eleanor's. And Eleanor wasn't going anywhere. No one was going anywhere. The world shut down for a week. And with the power knocked out—we were an all-electric household—the temperature inside plummeted.

Meanwhile, my dazed colleague was climbing out of his car. It had come to rest on its side against a vertical pipe from a former road sign in the Allens' ditch. The large limb from the oak, shattered into several large pieces, lay between us like a barricade, blocking the road. Ice and water made the ditches impossible to cross. I was trapped in my own front yard by my very own moat! The only way out was to slide down the driveway. But I fell, covering the last few feet on my ass.

Seeing me coming, my colleague waved a hand to show he was okay.

"I'll get my chainsaw!" I called. "We've got to clear the road for the EMTs!"

But the power was out. An electric chainsaw was useless. So I crawled back up the driveway on my hands and knees to fetch my axe and bow saws from the garage. Which is when Elaine opened the door from the kitchen.

"The basement's flooding!" she said. "The sump pump's out!"

Then—in the clarity that often comes from lack of sleep—the old eggbeater began whirring.

"Roll up the carpets down there," I said calmly, "and sandbag the well of the sump pump. Then bail the water into those old metal garbage cans."

The sump pump well was an open cylinder in the far corner of the basement—about five feet deep and three feet wide—with tile drains leading to the septic system. The sump pump itself, out of commission without electricity, sat at the bottom, the water slowly rising above it to spread across the concrete floor. Had I known that the power would be out for a week, I'd have told Elaine to light a candle and relax, because fighting that flood was useless. The basement—which extended beneath the family room and boys' bedrooms, with a crawl space beneath the rest of the house—would have several inches of water by the weekend. Fortunately, it was an unfinished basement. But the icy water would finish off all the stuff in boxes that were touching the floor.

Those two metal garbage cans in the basement held fireplace kindling—twigs and branches collected each year when the Rocky Mountain wind snapped them from the smaller swamp maples. Newspapers stored in the garage ignited this kindling in our fireplace, igniting in turn larger logs from the large swamp maples. But the kindling—soaked in the flood when dumped from the garbage cans—wouldn't catch, and the newspaper burned too quickly to provide sustained heat. So we sat there shivering in front of the fireplace beneath layers of long johns and winter coats, as the temperature in the house, worsened by the wind, sank below fifty.

"I'm freeeeezing!" Elaine said.

" . . . sunnuvabitch kindling!"

After the fourth sleepless night of huddling in bed together, knees knocking and teeth chattering, we couldn't take it any longer. Fortunately, the roads were finally opening. Which meant we could go for a drive in the heat of the car! A Chevy Caprice had replaced the Nova by then, so we opened the garage door with the manual release and slid capriciously down the driveway into County Road 50, which was freshly sanded and salted, and drove off in search of a cup of hot coffee.

But no restaurants were open. Their roofs had collapsed under the weight of ice and snow, or water damage had closed them. Gas stations were closed, too, since power had not been restored. Fortunately, the Caprice had a full tank.

So we drove on, picking up I-75 in Lima and heading toward Dayton. Incredibly, south of Hardin County, you could see exactly where the ice storm had crossed Ohio—a clear line where, quite abruptly, the trees were no longer white with ice, but black, with all limbs intact. Power lines stretched across the horizon instead of draping the ground.

Elaine was jubilant. "There's a motel! Let's get a room! That restaurant's open!"

Just then, for the first time in a week, the sun broke through the afternoon clouds. Of course, in our haste to abandon the house for the warmth of the car, we'd never thought of suitcases, toothbrushes, or a change of clothes.

"I want my shampoo," Elaine cried. "And hairdryer. I haven't showered in days!"

"Let's get something to eat," I said, "then go back to the house for what we need. We can return to the motel later and stay as long as we like."

So we drove back up I-75 to Lima and cut over to County Road 50. Where a crew from the electric company was restringing the lines.

Yard Wars of the Ohio Outback

Fairy Tales

At the start of our second spring on County Road 50, I confronted the grass. Which needed confronting.

The first task was to reseed the path that the previous owner's dog had worn across the side yard, running back and forth parallel to the road in its pen, chasing cars and joggers it could never catch. It was a long dirt trough, really, so determined had that dog been in getting nowhere.

Taking my wheelbarrow back to the cornfield, I skimmed some topsoil (what I borrowed in dirt I repaid in leaves each fall, a natural filler and fertilizer) and trundled it into the yard to fill that dog track. Then I seeded it with Kentucky Bluegrass, raked it smooth, and watered it with an adjustable lawn sprinkler I'd bought along with the grass seed at Furrows—the kind you attach to a garden hose with a special setting that could produce a long and narrow flow of water.

While the sprinkler was watering the dog strip, I attacked a bunch of small bare spots around the yard, each no bigger than the wide-brimmed straw hat I wore to protect my skin from the sun. I tilled these spots a few inches deep, sowed them with bluegrass, and watered them by hand, using a plastic sprinkling can. So far, so good.

Until the next morning, that is. When I found the reseeded bare spots torn up by some nocturnal animal that I'd actually accommodated by tilling the soil. Apparently too lazy to do its own digging, whatever-it-was caused me to repair the damage left in its wake—retilling, re-seeding, and raking those spots smooth again. This continued for three nights in a row, followed by my repairs in the morning.

"Something's looking for grubs," the head of the Biology Department told me.

"Something's pissing me off," was all I said. Ironically, the nocturnal critter was leaving the long dog track untouched.

"That's because of the lingering dog scent," the biologist said.

Had Chip and Lynn lived next door at the time, I would have invited them over with their seven dogs, giving the run of the yard to Big Mama, Bark, Yip, Yap, Yak, Yipe, and Yelp—letting them piss all over the place and leave their dog scent on my Kentucky Bluegrass to ward off the nocturnal grub-digger. But Chip and Lynn hadn't moved in yet. There were only cats next door. Which came over to shit in the driveway.

I never discovered the identity of that nocturnal digger—it may have been a skunk, raccoon, or possum, although I'd add another animal to those suspects much later. But I *did* discover a way to curb its digging. The previous owner had left an old refrigerator in the garage, which we didn't use because it didn't work. So I pressed its rectangular racks into service. They were just long enough and wide enough to cover the reseeded bare spots, separating them from the nocturnal digger like bars on a jail window. And so, for the first time in a week, the reseeded bare spots went unmolested.

"Those things look awful out there," Elaine said. "They glint in the sun."

"But they work!"

As soon as the seed had germinated and the grass had grown a few inches, I removed those refrigerator racks, and the spots continued undisturbed. The only problem was that the refrigerator had just four racks, and there were many bare spots. So I pressed the rectangular grill rack from our hibachi into service as well—it was spring, and we only grilled in the summer—rotating it randomly with the refrigerator racks from spot to spot on a nightly basis, creating a game of chance for the grub-digger.

A game I won when it went digging elsewhere.

. . .

But I couldn't win the dandelion war.

The problem with living in northwest Ohio is that in springtime the countryside fills up with dandelions before the farm fields are plowed and planted. Thousands of dandelions danced like a yellow sea along County Road 50 to the west of us. Which meant, of course, that their fluffy seeds were constantly blowing our way on the prevailing west wind. Leonine heads began popping up in April, and by the end of the month you couldn't see the green in the yard for all the yellow.

So off I went to Furrows for a spreader and five twenty-pound bags of Weed-'n'-Feed, which I spread across the yard in even rows. Well, I *thought* I'd spread it evenly—until the first good rain and a few days of sun. After which the yard was striped like a Bengal tiger. Rows of dark green grass now alternated with light green. Through which the dandelions poked their bright-yellow heads as if to mock me.

Goddam sunnuvabitch . . . !

Too impatient to wait for the Weed-'n'-Feed to take effect, I drove back to Furrows and returned with two sixteen-ounce plastic squirt bottles of Ortho Weed-B-Gone Max. "Results in 24 hours," the label boasted. "New foaming action! Kills over 200 weeds! One hundred percent root kill! Exclusive lawn-guard formula! Keep out of reach of children!" The only one of those 200 weeds depicted on the label was a dandelion—two yellow heads in full bloom and a third closed like an anus. All three extending from a base of raggedy leaves.

I could have purchased the Ortho Weed-B-Gone Max in a one-gallon container to which a handy gun was attached by a thin plastic hose. But it was too heavy to lug around the yard. I preferred the two-gun approach—twin sixteen-ounce plastic squirt bottles notched to fit your hand like a Colt .45, with an easy plastic trigger and adjustable spout that could spray foam or produce a bulletlike trajectory. I set mine to the latter and roamed the yard like Wyatt Earp, two guns blazing, firing left and right, shooting each of those yellow varmints right between the eyes. A day or two later those dandelions curled up and withered in agony. It was immensely satisfying.

But this approach required daily showdowns—I could shoot only the dandelions bold enough to lift their heads. And since they matured at different rates, there were always more waiting to bloom, like that anus in the picture on the label. So these daily gunfights went on for weeks. Until Adrian asked a simple question.

"Dad, what are those dark circles in the grass?"

. . .

While I was concentrating on the dandelions, dark concentric circles had appeared throughout the yard like strange signals to UFOs. I hadn't noticed them in the sea of yellow and the green-and-not-so-green stripes. But with the dandelions shriveling up, the rings were plainly visible.

"What now?" Elaine said.

"They look like giant archery targets," Owen said.

Each concentric ring within the circles ranged in width from six inches to two feet. Some of them spun off in exotic swirls like the great spiral nebula in Andromeda.

"Those are basidiomycetes," the head of the Biology Department told me, "a type of fungus. It grows out from a central point beneath the ground in a threadlike mass called mycelium. The popular name for them is fairy rings."

"We've got fairies?"

"Those green rings come from the nitrogen that's produced where the mycelium has died."

"We've got fairies!" I told the family at supper.

"Cool!" Owen said.

"Can they hurt you?" Adrian wanted to know.

"Not if I feed them."

So off I went to Furrow's for five twenty-pound bags of fungicide. Which, like the Weed-'n'-Feed, I spread in my new spreader. But as soon as the fairies were under control, the mole war began.

. . .

Or maybe they were voles. Whichever they were, they were doing donuts around the backyard. Large figure-eights as well, in long trails that always began at the edge of the cornfield, worked their way toward the pool, then went once or twice around the apple trees before reaching a dead end. Which is exactly what I had in mind for those moles. Or voles.

"The poor vole gets no recognition," the head of the Biology Department said. "But everybody knows about moles."

Voles, a kind of meadow mouse, construct visible tunnels about two inches wide just below the surface as they eat the roots of your grass. Moles, however, produce two types of subterranean runways. One—similar to the voles' feeding tunnel—appears as raised ridges in the lawn. The other—much deeper—allows the moles to unite their feeding tunnels in a network. The soil excavated from these tunnels is what you find in your lawn. Piled up in little volcanolike mounds.

"If you've got those little volcanolike mounds," the head of the Biology Department said, "you've got moles."

And we had those little volcanolike mounds.

It was about this time that new neighbors moved into the Allens' farmhouse across the street. Sadly, both Bob and Falita Allen had passed away since we'd moved to County Road 50, replaced by Neal and Amy—Amy was the Allens' granddaughter—whose three children, born in the next few years, we would watch grow up. Neal was a man's man, as tall as me but about fifty pounds more muscular. A man of guns. He came over once with a rifle to shoot a raccoon that had taken up residence in the large pipe beneath the mouth of our driveway. And a man of mole traps.

The device he offered looked like a medieval instrument of torture. It consisted of four vertical spikes in a kind of croquet wicket that you placed above the corkscrewing mole trails. Neal placed it, because the spring on that thing was so terrifically tight that I couldn't budge it to set it. But Neal did so with ease, as I gleefully imagined those wicked spikes skewering the little brains of our destructive underground engineers.

But in the days to come those moles never once set off that device. They were supposed to bump their heads on a metal trip thingy that touched the top of their tunnels. But I guess they learned how to duck. Like me mowing under the white pine out front.

What to do? I was afraid Owen and Adrian would get curious about that mole trap and spike their own hands. Or that the neighbors' cats would set it off and impale their paws. So I set it off myself with a stick—*wham!*—and it banged shut like a bear trap. Then I returned it to Neal with thanks and apologies.

Frustrated, I returned to Furrows, where the clerk gave me a knowing smile and held up a canister of Bonide Moletox. "Trusted since 1926," the label said. "Poison bait for use against Moles and Pocket Gophers in lawns, golf courses, and other non-crop areas. Also helps to protect bulbs at Fall Planting." But it was spring and I was planting grass seed. And fighting fairies and dandelions. And the last thing I needed was moles.

"This is what you need," the clerk assured me, sounding for all the world like the clerk at the pool-supply store. But it wasn't what I needed because it didn't work. It was a pain in the ass to apply anyway, given the lengthy instructions.

Prior to treatment determine which burrows are active according to one of the following two methods. Either press down a small section of the tunnel or remove a one-inch section of the tunnel's roof. Mark these sections and recheck in 24 hours. The burrow is considered active if the flattened runway has been raised up or if the roof has been repaired. Only treat active burrows.

Then things got complicated.

Carefully punch a hole in the top of the active tunnels, drop in a teaspoonful of Moletox and carefully close the hole with sod or stone. Do not collapse the runway again or allow loose soil to cover the bait. After two days check to see if the burrows are still active according to one of the two methods described above. If so, repeat treatment.

But that wasn't all.

Remove center plug from the conical mounds [what center plug?] with aid of a long-handled spoon and drop a teaspoonful of Moletox into the underground tunnel. Close opening with rock or soil. [What happened to the sod or stone above?] Do not allow loose dirt to cover bait.

Losing patience, I sprinkled the stuff in the volcanoes and trails willy-nilly. Then I walked around the yard, putting one foot in front of the other as if taking a sobriety test, squashing every last inch of those mole trails. Which, of course, rose again—like long and grassy loaves of bread—by the end of the week.

I was livid.

. . . *sunnuvabitch moles!*

So I returned to Furrows to purchase something I'd noticed on an earlier trip: a garden fork with a handle like a coal shovel and tines like the pitchfork in the famous painting by Grant Wood. Except that its tines were flatter and slightly less curved. Then, beginning at the edge of the cornfield, I worked my way through every mole-made donut, spiral, and corkscrew all the way to the pool and apple trees— inch by inch, stepping on that garden fork to sink its tines into the softened earth, replicating the action of Neal's medieval mole trap.

And each time I pulled that garden fork from the earth, I examined its tines for mole blood. Which, to my immense satisfaction, I found frequently.

It worked so well I told the clerk at Furrows that they should change the name of that garden tool to "mole fork."

. . .

Next to come, in that second spring on County Road 50 and all springs to follow, were the ants—little brown ants, red fire ants, big black ants—listed here in order of size.

As for their anatomy, one might adapt a line of Latin from Julius Caesar's report on Gaul: *Omnes formicae sunt divisue in tres partes*— head, thorax, and abdomen—although I'd always thought that *for-mica* meant tabletop, not ant. Regardless of color and size, however, they were all pests. And the first two kinds drove me mad.

I discovered the little brown ants while mowing the lawn. Like the moles, they created granular volcanoes that you couldn't miss. I'd roar over them with the Lawn Boy, squash them with my foot in passing, and the next day they'd be right back in business. It amused me at first, because of a poem I'd written—way back in junior high—about ants:

I squashed an anthill
Just for spite
To watch the ants

With all their might
Build it back
Grain by grain
For me to laugh
And squash again.

Which is what happened—time and again—out in the yard. But I never attacked the ants until the fire ants attacked *me* when I stepped into the cornfield in search of a golf ball. I'd gotten into the habit of hitting golf balls in the yard, setting up at the edge of the ditch and aiming at the pole on which the bluebird house sat, seventy-five yards distant, right on the edge of the cornfield. On this particular day I was wearing sandals instead of my golf shoes, and the instant I stepped into the mound of red fire ants I knew it—*YEOWW!*

Goddam . . . ants!

They stung me to pieces, teaching me a cruel lesson about the source of their name. My foot swelled immediately as those ants clamped their mandibles, causing me to kick off my sandals and run for the garden hose to cool my fiery skin. After which I immediately headed to Furrows, returning with a sixteen-ounce cardboard canister of Spectrum Ant Powder, a fine white powder with the active ingredient deltamethrin (.04%), among other ingredients (99.96%). I took comfort in just how little deltamethrin the stuff contained—an indication of its lethal toxicity—as well as the prefix *delta*. I figured the chemical concoction had been developed for the deltas down south, where those red fire ants held sway. Now I intended to knock them back there all the way from Ohio.

While I was at it, I figured I'd get rid of those little brown ants as well.

The label on the Spectrum Ant Powder canister listed all of the ants it combated—"Argentine, Southern, Field, Allegheny Mound, Florida Carpenter, Black Carpenter, Cornfield, Honey, Pavement, Red Imported Fire Ant, and Nuisance." That last category killed me. They *all* were nuisances as far as I was concerned. And I had the perfect treatment, with simple instructions for a change: "Sprinkle powder in a 12-inch band around the anthill or mound. Gently water treated areas."

I didn't bother with the big black ants because they confined themselves to the bark of the swamp maples. I'd seen ants like that as a kid.
We used to light "punks"—cattails on a stalk—and burn those black
suckers, just to see them curl up and shrivel. But on County Road 50
it was the red fire ants, and their annoying brown cousins, that fired
me up. So I sprinkled the white powder in a solid twelve-inch circle
around the anthills and mounds, gently watered the treated areas,
and waited.

I didn't check on the fire ant mound because I didn't want to take
any chances. It was easier to stay out of the cornfield. But the white
powder worked wonders on the little brown ants. They immediately
packed up and moved—only to reappear some thirty feet away a
day or two later. So I sprinkled the white powder in a twelve-inch
circle around the new anthills, gently watered the treated areas, and
waited. And the same thing happened. The powder didn't kill them.
It just made them relocate.

Goddam sunnuvabitch ants!

But I had to hand it to those little buggers. They were smart enough
to move from an adverse environment—just as we had moved from
Christopher Circle into the country.

"All those white spots look awful out there," Elaine said. "Like
150-yard markers on a golf course."

She had a point. So back I went to Furrows. Where the clerk, of
course, had just what I needed—Triazicide Soil & Turf Insect Killer
Granules—not white powder but brown granules. Same color as the
anthills! It killed ants along with everything else, from armyworms
to weevils. And it came with a strident warning on the label—
"Hazardous to humans and domestic animals."

Suddenly I felt like Harry Truman when presented with the atom
bomb.

But all it did was make those brown ants move again.

The Way to Winesburg

Winesburg, Ohio, Sherwood Anderson's classic short story collection that functions as a novel, is the book by which the literary world has come to know the small-town Midwest. It ranks twenty-fourth on the Modern Library list of the 100 best novels of the twentieth century.

The fictional town of Winesburg is based on Clyde, where Anderson spent the formative years of his boyhood. Today a small city with a population of 6,143, Clyde lies in north-central Ohio, eighty miles west of Cleveland and eighteen miles south of Lake Erie.

As you approach from the south on State Route 101, you'll suddenly see acres of apple trees in the surrounding farmland. Apples from these orchards, Anderson writes, are "put in barrels and shipped to the cities where they will be eaten in apartments that are filled with books, magazines, furniture, and people."

The gnarled and twisted apples left unpicked are like some of the characters we meet in Winesburg. Anderson calls them "grotesques." Yet each rejected apple, he notes, possesses a sweet spot, and few people "know the sweetness of the twisted apples."

As State Route 101 becomes South Main, a school appears on the left at the corner of Fair Street. This is the site of the former Clyde Fairgrounds, where every fall in the late nineteenth and early twentieth century—the era depicted in *Winesburg, Ohio*—"an American town worked terribly at the task of amusing itself." *Terribly* because, in those innocent days before the birth of modern industrialism, the county fair was the only game in town.

It is at the fairgrounds one summer day that Kate Swift, a thirty-year-old Winesburg schoolteacher, sits in the grass with her former student, the young George Willard, discussing his future. George, just eighteen, plans to become a writer. He is working as a reporter for the *Winesburg Eagle,* and the townsfolk gravitate to him with their personal stories, as if sensing he is destined for greatness. Kate, who has traveled in Europe and lived in New York City, senses this too, but her concern only confuses the young George.

At the far end of the Clyde Fairgrounds a hill descends in an open sward to Waterworks Pond. Covered with dense bushes and trees in Anderson's day, it is here that George Willard finds himself one evening with Belle Carpenter, who works at a millinery shop in town. Awakening to the power of manhood, George is determined that Belle take him seriously. But she is in love with Ed Handby, a Winesburg bartender whom she teases to fits of jealousy. Ed has been following the pair and interrupts them, knocking his rival to the ground repeatedly, and the humiliating confrontation shatters George's burgeoning self-confidence.

The validation of maturity that George is seeking eventually comes to him at this very spot, in the company of Helen White—banker's daughter, college freshman, and maiden jewel of Winesburg. Helen is home from college for the county fair with one of her instructors, but she manages to leave him with her mother at nightfall and slip off to meet George. Together they sit in the empty grandstand at the fairgrounds, each aware of the growing sophistication of the other. They kiss, but, "that impulse did not last." Instead, they retreat to the crest of the hill at Waterworks Pond, escaping their mutual embarrassment by slipping into "the animalism of youth"—playfully pushing and shoving one another on the hillside.

The former fairgrounds lie along the brow of a low hill rising from a shallow valley that cuts through Clyde from east to west. The valley follows a stream formed by Sucker Run and Raccoon Creek on their way to Waterworks Pond. This stream becomes Wine Creek in *Winesburg, Ohio.* And Clyde's South Street, which skirts Waterworks

Pond, becomes Winesburg's Sucker Road, where Kate Swift, driven by conflicting passions for George Willard, walks in a delirious state one stormy winter night.

Turn left on Fair Street from State Route 101 and Spring Avenue is the first street on the right. At 129 Spring sits a narrow two-story frame house that dates to the nineteenth century. This was the Anderson residence circa 1888–95. Before that the family lived for about a year in a bungalow at 214 Race Street beyond Waterworks Pond. Both residences gave Anderson ready access to Waterworks Pond and the fairgrounds, to which we return time and again in *Winesburg, Ohio*.

Maxine Dunigan, a spunky five-foot-two octogenarian, has lived at 129 Spring since the end of World War II, when her late husband Bill was in the navy. The house, she says, "is a humble dwelling, and a bit run down." The only item they found on the premises linked to Anderson himself was a gas lamp Bill Dunigan donated to Clyde's Winesburg Inn, a popular restaurant that closed in the early 1990s.

Although hundreds of people have dropped by to ask about Anderson over the decades, I'm the first in the last five years. But the welcome is warm.

"The first time I read *Winesburg, Ohio*," Maxine Dunigan says, "I found Anderson to be a very adventuresome soul. Yet I've heard that members of the Clyde Library once held a party to burn his books!"

Obviously there were some sour apples among the gnarled and twisted ones in town when *Winesburg, Ohio* was published in 1919. Certain residents claimed to recognize themselves in Anderson's stories, and their descendants still live in Clyde. The names are well known but surrendered guardedly, probably because—as the late literary critic Malcolm Cowley wrote in his introduction to *Winesburg, Ohio*—the book was once attacked as "pessimistic," "destructive," and "morbidly sexual."

Cowley viewed it, instead, as "a work of love, an attempt to break down the walls that divide one person from another," as well as a "celebration of small-town life." As if to acknowledge that fact, the Clyde Public Library on West Buckeye Street, two blocks north of Spring Avenue, today houses a Sherwood Anderson collection.

Not all moments in *Winesburg, Ohio* are dark ones. The eccentric Joe Welling, who lived "in a little grove of trees beyond where the Main

Street of Winesburg crossed Wine Creek," more than lives up to his name, welling up with enthusiasm when "beset by ideas" and but-tonholing people to explain them. Joe discovers, for example, that the "water is up in Wine Creek," but it hasn't been raining in Winesburg. Nonetheless, the water's risen to within eleven and a half inches of the bridge flooring—Joe's measured it himself, with a ruler from the hardware store in town. Why the high water? It's been raining "over in Medina County," Joe explains. "That's where Wine Creek comes from. Everyone knows that."

I didn't, but I checked it out, and Joe's right—Medina County lies to the east of Clyde—which is why I've often stepped into Wine Creek myself, where it passes beneath Spring Avenue just beyond Maxine Dunigan's, whipping a ruler from my back pocket to measure the distance between the water and the bridge, much to the dismay of the college students on my literature field trips. Joe Welling had a habit of shocking his listeners to make a point. I like to do the same.

A right turn at the end of Spring and a short walk along Cherry Street returns you to Main. One block further north and a left on West Forest takes you to the Presbyterian church, just fifty yards in. Built in 1869, the brick structure has a bell tower above the entrance at the right front corner. The tower was added in 1891 and renovated in 1960, and the tower study—that of Reverend Curtis Hartman in *Winesburg, Ohio*—is still in use.

When from his study Reverend Hartman discovers that he can look into the upstairs bedroom of Kate Swift— observing her night after night until he sees her naked—he is propelled into a paroxysm of lust and guilt with few parallels in American literature. The two-story frame dwelling that used to stand beside the tower was removed for a parking lot in the 1980s, but it once stood as close to the church as does the house that remains on the left.

David Gowen, the current pastor, came to the Presbyterian church two and a half years ago to begin a second career after thirty-two years at Ford. Before that, he'd never heard of Clyde, let alone *Wines-burg, Ohio*. At Ford, before he was commissioned as a lay pastor, he served as chaplain to the union.

"I'm not from the area," he says, "and so *Winesburg, Ohio* is not in my blood. Nor is my congregation engulfed in the whole Winesburg thing." Still, he read the book when he learned of its connection to Clyde, found it a "good read," and considers Anderson "very talented." Although he's never had the occasion to use *Winesburg, Ohio* in any of his sermons, he has mentioned the book during church coffee hours.

Gowen was up in the tower study when I first telephoned him. It was early February, and he found it "awfully cold up there." Ironically, so did Reverend Hartman on the winter nights when he was watching Kate Swift, before a revelation sent him running to the *Winesburg Eagle* to announce to George Willard, "God has manifested himself to me in the body of a woman."

When I asked Gowen if he'd ever experienced any "vibes" up in the famous tower, he recounted one incident in particular that he sees as both "odd" and "spectacular." It was summer, and the tower window above the parking lot was open when he heard a commotion down below. Stepping to the window, where he remained hidden behind its screen, he saw a woman trying to control four young children, one of whom was about to dart out into the street. Just as he did so, Gowen's voice thundered from above: *"Stop right there!"* The boy stopped in his tracks, looked up, then retreated to the woman with his hand extended.

"I scared the crap out of that little critter," Gowen says. The incident became the theme of one of his sermons—*Stop right there.*

Rachel Dewey, a third-year law student at Ohio Northern University, grew up in Clyde and was baptized in the Presbyterian church, two blocks from her parents' home on Main Street. She remembers "roaming around" up in the tower after church services when she was seven years old. Dewey read *Winesburg, Ohio* in junior high, when it appeared as an option on a reading list. Her initial response was, "Wow! This is neat! It's right here in town!"

She often discussed the book with her parents. "I was struck by the creepy characters and the dark vision of life. It portrayed the people as crazy and loony, but that's not how it is. We're part of the history of Clyde."

By *we* she means the Dewey family, four generations of Clyde attorneys. Her father, a local judge who has worked with the Clyde Museum, has his offices right on Main Street. After graduation, Rachel will become the fifth-generation family lawyer in town. One of her ancestors, Thomas Payne Dewey (1852–1931), helped establish Clyde's first telephone company. Lawyers are mentioned only briefly in *Winesburg, Ohio*, but very positively. Joe Welling's father, for example, was "a man of some dignity in the community, a lawyer and a member of the state legislature in Columbus."

Rachel Dewey likens Clyde's reaction to *Winesburg, Ohio* to that of the 1990 film *Welcome Home, Roxy Carmichael*, about a famous Clyde celebrity whose return home sends the locals into a frenzy. Her father's Main Street offices can be glimpsed in one scene, but, as Dewey says, "the film makes the people seem strange." *Welcome Home, Roxy Carmichael*, starring Winona Ryder, was written by Karen Leigh Hopkins, who grew up in Sandusky, Ohio, less than twenty miles from Clyde, and the parallels with Sherwood Anderson are obvious.

The parking lot beside the Presbyterian church offers a shortcut to the rear of the Clyde Museum at 124 West Buckeye Street, converted from an Episcopal church built in 1886. Enter at the front and proceed along the nave, and there's a modest display devoted to Anderson on the left.

Materials among the Anderson memorabilia include an article from the August 29, 1926, edition of the *Sandusky Register* and a reprint of a 1967 leaflet from the Sandusky County Historical Society. Biographical notes on Anderson are provided by the late Thaddeus Hurd, an old friend of the Anderson family who returned to Clyde in the nineteen seventies to spur a major effort to renew interest in *Winesburg, Ohio*, copies of which are for sale at the museum. Hurd's 1988 map for a walking tour of Anderson-related sites is also available. It's the guide on which I have based my many field trips.

The Clyde Museum opens for the season in April, but museum officials can be contacted any time through the Clyde Heritage League. One member, local historian Ralph Rogers, has often opened the museum for my students. He's a ready source of information about Sherwood Anderson, his extensive local knowledge reminiscent of the tidbits of news that it was George Willard's job to gather as a reporter for the *Winesburg Eagle*.

In *Winesburg, Ohio* Helen White lives on Buckeye Street, the same street where the museum and library are located. Helen's father,

Banker White, had built "a huge brick house" there, like the one right beside the museum. The White home is finer than the house that "had at one time been the show place of the town"—the home of Seth Richmond, George Willard's rival for the affections of Helen White. "The Richmond place was in a little valley far out at the end of Main Street. Farmers coming into town by a dusty road from the south passed by a grove of walnut trees, skirted the Fairgrounds with its high board fence covered with advertisements, and trotted their horses down through the valley past the Richmond place into town."

Seth Richmond, who is a year or two younger than George, forms the third side of a love triangle with George and Helen. As a schoolgirl, Helen had a crush on Seth, but George, newly employed at the *Winesburg Eagle,* naively sends Seth to talk to Helen on his behalf. He is determined to fall in love with her so he can write a love story. "See what she says to that," George tells Seth. "See how she takes it, and then you come and tell me." The plan almost backfires on George, as Seth and Helen achieve a tacit intimacy, but nothing comes of it, preparing the way for George and Helen to discover each other.

Buckeye Street is the scene of another awkward love triangle in *Winesburg, Ohio,* as the Reverend Curtis Hartman, in an attempt to put thoughts of Kate Swift out of his mind, "began to be something of a lover in the presence of his wife. One evening when they drove out together he turned the horse out of Buckeye Street," and after making their way to Waterworks Pond, "put his arm about Sarah Hartman's waist." The Hartmans' carriage ride would have taken them out the length of West Buckeye, where several stately Victorian homes are preserved today, a staid backdrop to the passions of yesteryear.

A left turn as you leave the museum will take you to the Clyde Public Library at 222 West Buckeye. Turn right and you're back on Main, the setting for much of the drama in *Winesburg, Ohio.*

On one occasion, "There had been an accident on Main Street. A team of horses had been frightened by a train and had run away. A little girl, the daughter of a farmer, had been thrown from a buggy and killed." Three of the four doctors in town respond to the call for help, but Doctor Parcival does not. In explaining himself to George Willard, Parcival reveals himself as a charlatan and hypocrite, if not a madman. He fears he'll be hanged for not rushing to the scene. Parcival wants to write a book, the point of which is "that everyone in the world is Christ and they are all crucified." He tells George, "If something happens, perhaps you will be able to write the book that I may never get written."

Today, the offices of the *Clyde Enterprise* are at 109 North Main, between Buckeye and Railroad Street, adjacent to the offices of Dewey & Dewey. In *Winesburg, Ohio* the *Clyde Enterprise* becomes the *Winesburg Eagle*, its office also on Main Street. According to Becky Brooks, the paper's editor for the last twelve years, it's "clear that local people make a connection between Anderson's *Eagle* and the local 'real' paper, which started 131 years ago."

One night George Willard leaves the *Winesburg Eagle* for a rendezvous with the promiscuous Louise Trunnion. Once he's lost his virginity, he parades up and down Main Street, feeling "pleased" and "satisfied" with himself and wanting "more than anything else to talk to some man." Yet he nervously senses the sordid nature of his adventure.

Jeanette Weisz, Becky Brooks's niece, has lived in Clyde since she was ten. She read some of the stories in *Winesburg, Ohio* as a junior at Clyde High School, the traditional year for American literature. Initially, she "didn't care" that they were related to Clyde. Then she read the whole book. "It's weird that some old people are still touchy about the subject," she said. "Clyde is the kind of town where the names are always there. And the speculation continues. But why make a big deal? I find it interesting that the book was banned, and now we have Winesburg Christmas Weekend."

Weisz's Aunt Becky is the current chairperson for Winesburg Christmas Weekend. She says that local businesses such as the Winesburg Motel, Winesburg Mortgage Company, and the former Winesburg Inn "picked up the Winesburg moniker, but the names and stories behind the book had little to do with them."

Winesburg Christmas Weekend, the first in December, is a modern throwback to the county fair in *Winesburg, Ohio*. "Originally," Brooks says, "the idea was to dress in the era of the book—the nineteen hundreds—to celebrate the old-fashioned ideas of the Christmases residents remembered from childhood. But it's no surprise I get calls from the region asking why Clyde calls its Christmas festival 'Winesburg Christmas.'"

Not everyone is aware of the Winesburg bandwagon. And not everyone's on it. Brooks's grandfather, who lived in the township adjoining Clyde, once told Brooks that he "had no use for Anderson." He said he and others knew the people Anderson had been writing about and truly disliked the man. As Brooks says, "I believe Anderson was resented by many who believe he never found the village good enough and made his fortune at their expense." Brooks herself was interested in *Winesburg, Ohio* long before she moved to Clyde in 1992, having read the book for pleasure both in high school and college.

The Main Street of Winesburg is the scene of some minor dramas that carry importance in the life of any small town. Turk Smollett, the local half-wit, goes out of his way to trundle a wheelbarrow of boards through town, proud of the way he can balance the load. And on the day that George Willard departs Winesburg by train, "wondering what he would find at the end of his journey," Helen White "came running along Main Street hoping to have a parting word with him, but he had found a seat and did not see her."

The Clyde depot—between Railroad Street and the current tracks on North Main—no longer exists, but its fictional counterpart appears frequently in *Winesburg, Ohio*. According to Brooks, "Thaddeus Hurd and his friends dedicated a Sherwood Anderson Park in the center of downtown in the depot area mentioned in the book, but the original railroad tracks are gone, as is the building. The depot area is now city parking. The city added an Anderson Street five or six years ago, but if you ask people here what famous Anderson came from Clyde, most would say Tim Anderson, who played for the Buffalo Bills and is now with the Atlanta Falcons."

By the time George Willard departs Winesburg by train, we are familiar with the depot. On the station platform during strawberry season, "men and boys loaded boxes of the red, fragrant berries into two express cars that stood upon the siding." And Seth Richmond, disgusted with George Willard and his designs on Helen White, seeks solace there. "Crossing a little dusty street and climbing a low iron railing, he went to sit upon the grass in the station yard." A triangle of grass remains at the site today, providing a perfect place to sit and reflect on *Winesburg, Ohio*.

In one of Anderson's stories, however, the depot is the scene of an ignominious defeat for George Willard, akin to his pummeling by Ed Handby. Summoned in the middle of the night to the station by Elmer Cowley, an inarticulate youth who is jealous of George and has stolen money from his own father in order to leave town, George is summarily beaten "half unconscious" on the platform before Elmer springs aboard a passing train, his violent escape in stark contrast to George's later leave-taking.

In another story, the railroad station is the point of departure for a grisly event involving old Windpeter Winters, "who was looked upon by everyone in Winesburg as a confirmed old reprobate." As Anderson writes, "People from the part of Northern Ohio in which Winesburg lies will remember old Windpeter by his unusual and tragic death." Winters got drunk in town and decided to drive home along the railroad tracks, lashing his team of horses headlong into an oncoming locomotive.

Anderson exacts a subtle truth from this violent moment: "Boys like young George Willard and Seth Richmond will remember the incident quite vividly because, although everyone in our town said that the old man would go straight to hell and that the community was better off without him, they had a secret conviction that he knew what he was doing and admired his foolish courage. Most boys have seasons of wishing they could die gloriously instead of just being grocery clerks and going on with their humdrum lives."

Just north of the former depot, adjacent to a chiropractor's office at 112 West Maple, is the parking lot Brooks mentioned. It occupies the site of the former Empire House Hotel, which became the model for the shabby New Willard House. Run by George Willard's parents, the New Willard House is the scene of dramatic confrontations between George and his mother and father. Anderson's parents never ran a hotel in Clyde, but the sad death of Elizabeth Willard in *Winesburg, Ohio* parallels the death of Anderson's own mother, when Anderson—like young George Willard—was just eighteen.

Across Main, out East Maple, is the McPherson Cemetery, where Anderson's mother, Emma Smith Anderson, is buried beside his father in Section 4, Lot 23. The short walk takes you by the site of a potentially dangerous confrontation in *Winesburg, Ohio* involving the eccentric Joe Welling, whom we left measuring the height of the water in Wine Creek. "Joe fell in love with Sarah King, a lean, sad-looking woman who lived with her father and brother in a brick house that stood opposite the gate leading to the Winesburg Cemetery."

The two King men are among the bad apples in town. Tom King "was reported to have killed a man before he came to Winesburg." Still, old Edward King "seemed more dangerous than his silent, fierce-looking son." So when Joe goes courting Sarah King, George Willard fears the outcome. But when confronted by the two Kings at the New Willard House, Joe overwhelms them with an idea for breeding new fruits and vegetables, should all the wheat, corn, oats, peas, and potatoes in the world ever get swept away. When last seen, the two Kings are walking quickly in order to keep up with Joe as he heads off to find Sarah. "Let's go up to your house," Joe says. "I want to tell her of this." A small old brick house on East Maple—just across Main from the depot—may have been the one Anderson had in mind as the King family home.

Not all stories in *Winesburg, Ohio* take place in town. Four involve Jesse Bentley, whose farm "was situated in a tiny valley watered by Wine Creek." A fanatic Christian who identifies himself with the ancient biblical patriarchs, Bentley buys up farms in the area, including "part of a long stretch of black swampland," and becomes wealthy by draining the swamps and planting cabbages and onions. His daughter and grandson live in Winesburg for a while, connecting Jesse's fate to various townsfolk. The four stories about Jesse comprise a novella within the longer book and offer a primer on Ohio pioneer history. They offer as well a striking lesson on the dangers of interpreting the Bible too literally.

Jennifer Pierce grew up in Clyde and remembers discussing *Winesburg, Ohio* in high school. She especially remembers "the story about the peeping Tom," Reverend Hartman. "Clyde's slogan," she says, "is 'America's Famous Small Town.' It's on a sign that greets you on Route 20, the McPherson Highway."

The phrase is also prominently displayed on Clyde's official Web site—*America's Famous Small Town*. But *famous for what?* you might ask. The site boasts that Clyde is "home to the world's largest washing machine manufacturer" (Whirlpool). It's also "the boyhood home of Major General James B. McPherson, highest ranking Union officer killed in the Civil War." But the fact that Clyde was the model for *Winesburg, Ohio* isn't mentioned.

In January of 2008, I wrote to Clyde's newly elected mayor to ask if he's read *Winesburg, Ohio* and, if so, what he thinks of it. I also asked if the omission of Anderson from the Web site is an oversight or a matter of policy. He didn't respond. Nor did I get a response from the current owner/occupant of the former Anderson home at 214 Race Street. Others in town, obviously, were more than willing to speak to me. Maxine Dunagin welcomed me into her home, and I climbed to the tower study of the Presbyterian church with Pastor Gowen.

A Clyde promotional brochure from the era of Thaddeus Hurd's Anderson revival, dances gingerly between past and present: "The famous American novelist, Sherwood Anderson, told the story of Clyde long ago in the novel *Winesburg, Ohio*. Come and hear the story of Clyde as it is today . . . we think you'll like what you hear."

In 2003 the Ohio Bicentennial Commission placed an Ohio Historical Marker dedicated to Anderson in the park at the depot. And Joe Stickney, retired English Department chairperson at Clyde High School, says that classroom sets of *Winesburg, Ohio* are available in the school bookroom. Current English teachers tell me they've read Anderson with their literature classes.

Clyde doesn't shy away from its literary heritage. Nonetheless, Anderson's legacy remains a double-edged sword for local residents, whom Pastor Gowen describes as "proud and protective."

I always end my field trips to Clyde at the grave of Anderson's mother in the McPherson Cemetery. Then we step onto the railroad tracks abutting the graveyard. The train on which George Willard leaves town "runs from Cleveland to where it connects with a great trunk line railroad with terminals in Chicago and New York." We know that Anderson himself took trains in both directions, and when heading east he would have passed right by his mother's grave. Keeping that in mind, I like to read aloud the final paragraph of *Winesburg, Ohio*, imagining George on the train as it leaves the depot:

The young man's mind was carried away by his growing passion for dreams. One looking at him would not have thought him particularly sharp. With the recollection of little things occupying his mind he closed his eyes and leaned back in the car seat. He stayed that way for a long time and when he aroused himself and again looked out of the car window the town of Winesburg had disappeared and his life there had become but a background on which to paint the dreams of his manhood.

Read *Winesburg, Ohio*, then visit Anderson's hometown, and you'll discover that the way to Winesburg is through your own backyard.

Yard Wars of the Ohio Outback
Squirrel Wars, the Video

Our squirrel wars on County Road 50 lasted seven years. But it seemed like a hundred. Which is why I sent for a shotgun.

I say seven because I initially thought Adrian's rock band was to blame. The band—known at first as D.F.E. (Disgruntled Former Employees), then Mighty Trees—began playing together during their sophomore year in high school and stayed together through college, rehearsing in our unfinished basement all the while. And so, when I first saw the nicks and gouges in the frame around the front door, I assumed they'd been caused by members of the band, inadvertently knocking against it with their guitar cases, drums, and amplifiers as they entered the house en route to the basement.

So I repainted the nicks and gouges and told the guys to be more careful. But the damage continued—even after the band began to enter the house through the garage, which gave more ready access to the basement from the family room. It was more than a year, however, before I requested this adjustment in point of entry. And when the nicks and gouges continued, I began to wonder.

The front door—a storm door with glass inserts in winter and screens in summer—opened into a small room with a single window that we called the mudroom. Eight feet long and five feet wide, the mudroom led to another storm door that protected the "official" entrance to the house. Curiously, the nicks and gouges in the external mudroom door frame never reached more than twenty inches high. But they did become more jagged over time, as if something was chewing away at the wood. In fact, something *was* chewing away at the wood. I just couldn't figure out what the hell it was. Three cement steps led to the mudroom from a small sidewalk at the top of our gravel driveway, one of which would soon add to the mystery.

I repaired the gnawed spots with plastic wood—which dried to a solid substance much harder than the wood itself—and repainted them. But the chewing (and plastic wood and repainting) continued. And I grew annoyed.

Goddam sunnuvabitch whatever-you-are!

Meanwhile, I discovered a colony of small brown ants living just inside the mudroom storm door, the sand of their anthill spilling from a corner pillar in the interior wall.

"Aha!" I said to Elaine. "I get it now! Those ants got tired of moving around the yard and set up shop in the mudroom! Now they're eating us out of house and home!"

"But they're not termites," Elaine said. "Nor are they carpenter ants."

She had a point. They were just "nuisance" ants, taking advantage of the nicks and gouges in the doorframe to come in out of the weather. Which is exactly what a mudroom is for.

And so began my first offensive tactic in the squirrel wars of County Road 50—mousetraps. I took half a dozen mousetraps from the pool shed and set them, unbaited, along the external cement ledge at the bottom of the mudroom doorframe, where whatever-it-was obviously stood on its hind legs while chewing the house. By morning, three of those traps—all to the right of the door—had been set off. So I reset them. And next time I checked, one of them had been ripped apart, its spring askew, with one of the two staples that held the snappy thingy to the little strip of wood missing. Apparently I had snagged whatever-it-was, however briefly, and whatever-it-was had been annoyed. And was strong enough to rip apart a mousetrap!

"I need heavier artillery," I told Elaine.

So I broke out the rattrap I'd used for the chipmunk on Christopher Circle, baited it with peanut butter, and set it behind the hedge, where I figured whatever-it-was was concealing itself en route to the mudroom for its daily chew.

But in the morning that rattrap was gone. Whatever-it-was had dragged it away—the trap must have caught it by the paw (or nose, I hoped)—leaving a trail through the dew in the grass. The trail led from behind the hedge, across the front yard, down into the ditch and out again, and then across the road into a field just west of Neal and Amy's yard.

The chewing-of-the-doorframe continued for several years, never higher than twenty inches. And while I was busy repairing the nicks and gouges with plastic wood and paint, a new development occurred—sandlike grains began to appear on the top step to the mudroom.

At first I simply swept those grains away with a broom. But they reappeared in a day or so. And when they continued to reappear, month after month, I finally realized where they were coming from—from the vertical face of the top step, just below the level of the mudroom floor. Something was scraping at the very center of that cement face, wearing it away methodically.

Two months after that discovery, I noticed a tiny pinhole in the face of the step. Which was subsequently enlarged to a peephole. Whatever-it-was was determined to scratch open a hole large enough to get inside!

Descending into the basement to reconnoiter, I removed a plywood panel in the wall above the washing machine and climbed into the crawl space, wearing basketball kneepads I used on the roof when removing leaves from the gutters. Then I brushed aside the cobwebs from the overhead floor joists and made my way beneath the living room toward the front of the house. But the crawl space abruptly ended at the cement foundation, a solid wall of poured concrete just short of the mudroom.

"At least whatever-it-is," I told Elaine, "can't get into the house from out front."

"Maybe we can identify it by the size of the hole it makes."

That hole was getting bigger and bigger. But I wasn't about to give whatever-it-was construction rights on my very own doorstep. So I went to Furrows for some Quikcrete, cracked through that hole with a hammer, and stood back, in case whatever-it-was was in there waiting to pounce. But all I found was the mudroom foundation—a wall of cinderblocks, the kind with holes, set like a row of office mailboxes—perfect for nest-building and concealing a litter of little whatever-it-was's. So I filled those holes with Quikcrete and refaced the step with a trowel.

In one of those cinderblocks I found a rusty Coke can, no doubt deposited by a member of the construction crew that had built the house. But I was beginning to believe it had been put there by whatever-it-was.

. . .

Time passed. And just when I began to think that whatever-it-was had left of its own accord, nicks and gouges appeared out front again. And my repairs continued.

One spring, as Elaine and I pulled into the driveway after dark, the headlights of the Caprice caught a large gray possum lying on the front step. *Aha! Whatever-it-was is a possum!* But the following summer the beam of my headlights caught a young raccoon creeping into the hedges beneath the picture window. *Aha! Whatever-it-was is a raccoon!*

The breakthrough finally came in broad daylight, when Elaine returned at noon from a morning shift at the Lima Library.

"It's a long red rat!" she said, telephoning me at my office on campus. "It slinked into the hedge from the front step as soon as I pulled into the driveway!"

"That's no rat," the head of the Biology Department said. "That's a Red Jimmy, the worst kind of squirrel. Their teeth grow constantly, and if they don't chew on something to file them down, they won't be able to eat. They'll chew *anything*—power lines, screens, even metal. They're powerful diggers as well."

I hurried home to check the Florida room, which, along with three large sliding glass windows on the south side, had two screened windows on the west. Sure enough—the corners of the screens were being eaten away. Defeated at the mudroom steps, the enemy was circling the house in an attempt to gain entry! Fortunately, we kept those windows shut against the prevailing wind and rain, so any breaking-and-entering rodent would get no farther than its own reflection in the glass.

. . . sunnuvabitch squirrels!

Suddenly it all seemed logical. I remembered the Olympic flame atop the telephone pole on the day we'd moved in. And the digging that had always followed my planting of grass seed, whether in spring or fall. A definite pattern had been emerging over the years—with two major causes.

The first needs explaining. Each year since moving in, we'd planted a Christmas tree between the pitcher's mound and rear property line. Meanwhile, the row of swamp maples on our eastern border had matured. And the two big swamp maples by our badminton court had doubled in size, despite regularly losing large branches to high winds. The apple trees had grown too, along with the willows (while they lasted). And other trees, mostly swamp maples and locusts, had sprung up in the yard and flourished.

After the ice storm, when surveying the yard damage for insurance purposes, I'd counted forty trees. In short, except for our ball field, which remained a wide-open green sward, our acre had become a shady park. Just perfect for squirrels. But why were they focusing on *our* yard? The answer—the second cause—was simple. By default. Because the neighborhood had literally gone to the dogs, a squirrel's natural enemy.

To our west, Big Mama, Bark, Yip, Yap, Yak, Yipe, and Yelp kept Chip and Lynn's property free of squirrels. Across the street to the north, Neal and Amy had moved in with one dog and then inherited another—a pregnant pit bull that, once it had littered, would charge me as I went out to the mailbox, as if I were going to cross the street to molest its puppies. Likewise, new neighbors now lived to the east of us, a young couple who would eventually raise two kids and five beagles. The incessant barking that surrounded us had driven all neighborhood squirrels into our dog-free shady acre.

I'd never really noticed any squirrels because I hadn't been looking. Squirrels hate noise, and so they'd skedaddle whenever I roared around the yard with the Lawn Boy. But that was fewer than three hours a week. The rest of the time they had the run of the place.

"Squirrels are quite amazing," the head of the Biology Department marveled. "The part of their brain for remembering details is well developed. They teach their young everything they learn. They'll actually carry their babies across a street to show them where food is, whether it's nuts or apples."

Apples? Suddenly I remembered the tooth marks on the Golden and Goddam Delicious that littered the ground every autumn.

"We've become a safe haven for terrorist rodents!" I told Elaine. "All these years they've been operating with impunity!"

Now I was ready to impugn them.

. . .

Chucking the mousetraps and rattraps (they'd been squirrel-chucked anyway), I broke out my trusty squirrel trap and set it outside Owen's bedroom, where I'd seen a bold Red Jimmy perched upside-down on the exterior wall one morning, exactly as you'd see a squirrel coming down a tree—stopping for an instant, tail in the air, head darting left and right—before continuing to the ground and running off. This one, startled by my sudden presence, paused long enough to look me in the eye, dismiss me with disdain, and scamper away toward the swamp maple at the rear of the badminton court.

That did it. I felt like Hrothgar taunted by Grendel. Which left me no choice but to become Beowulf.

Retreating into the house, I peanut-buttered the squirrel trap and placed it where that squirrel had descended. Next morning the trap lay on its side in the middle of the backyard—ransacked, its feeding pan askew. But the peanut butter was intact, having dried and stuck in place. The squirrel had knocked the trap for a loop in an effort to shake the peanut butter loose. Incredible!

Possessed by anger that bordered on paranoia, I piled apples like park cannonballs in every corner of the yard and heaved them at any squirrel in sight. I bought a pellet gun—a pistol type—at a yard sale and left it loaded in the Florida room, slipping outside whenever I saw a Red Jimmy in one of the trees. And when it darted out of sight on the far side of the trunk, I'd tiptoe closer, waiting for it to come around again in its descent. And then—*ping!*—I'd blast it point-blank.

But their skin was too thick to inflict damage. The pellet was akin to a bee sting. And the look those squirrels gave me was akin to condescension. *Is that the best you can do?* they seemed to be saying. Before they jumped from the tree and ran off.

. . . sunnuvabitch squirrels!

Year after year I'd drop whatever I was doing to run into the yard after squirrels, heaving apples or reaching for my pellet gun. Fearing for my mental health, Elaine returned from the library one night with a surprise—a forty-five-minute video called *Squirrel Wars*. The timing was uncanny, and I watched intently as the narrator, his tone alternating between candid amusement and distraught resignation, detailed the antics of squirrels. And their alleged antidotes.

Squirrel Wars showed rogue squirrels attacking birdfeeders and birdhouses. If you hung a birdfeeder from a horizontal metal wire, they'd hug that wire upside down, crawl to the bird feeder, and descend. The antidote? String the wire itself with plastic bottles, which roll and spin, causing the squirrels to fall off.

If you set a birdfeeder on a pole, that pole had better be eight feet high, because squirrels can leap as high as six feet straight up. If they climb the pole, you can grease it, or protect it with a baffle, a metal thingy that resembles the hat of a Vietnamese peasant.

But we had no birdfeeder. And the Red Jimmies weren't after our birdhouse. They were eating the very house we lived in!

One Harry Homeowner in the video had a similar problem, squirrels bedeviling his wooden deck. So he electrified it. Whenever squirrels chewed his deck, he'd slip by the dining room window and throw a switch, feeding them a jolt of electricity. But those sunnuvabitch squirrels soon learned that man-passing-window equals deck-giving-jolt. So they'd scamper off whenever they saw Harry through the dining room window.

Then Harry got himself a shotgun. But it went off accidentally and blew a hole in his dining room floor. Which is why *I* didn't send for a shotgun. Until I was overcome with desperation. Because there were no laws against guns in Hardin County.

"Only Hawaii and Australia don't have squirrels," I told Elaine. "That's what the video said. A shotgun's cheaper than moving."

"Cheaper than a funeral as well," was all she said.

. . .

But the shotgun cost me only the price of UPS shipping. Because my brother in Connecticut shipped me what had been hanging for years over his fireplace—our grandfather's shotgun—a .410 gauge, "nothin' but a peashooter," as ol' Gramps used to say. But it packed more of a punch than my pellet gun. As a kid, my father had hunted squirrels with that gun. And my brother and I had shot it ourselves when we were kids.

"The only problem," my brother said on the phone, "is that it hasn't been fired in ages." Which led to nightmares of it exploding in my face.

A week later ol' Gramps' .410 shotgun arrived in a long slim box packed with styrofoam popcorn, which I had to clean out of the barrel and from around the trigger, lending a credible basis to my nightmares.

"What if a piece of styrofoam clogs the works?" Elaine said. "You'll shoot your eye out!" She was trying to be funny, quoting a line from *A Christmas Story*, our favorite holiday film, about a boy who gets a BB gun for Christmas. But she was deadly serious and I knew it.

"It can't go off without ammo," I said lamely. But by the end of the week I had ammo—a box of shotgun shells purchased at a sporting goods store in Lima. Then fate intervened, as is its wont, sparing me from ever shooting that shotgun. Although it pitted me face to face with a Red Jimmy.

. . .

One of the maligned victims in *Squirrel Wars* had used peanuts as bait, whereas I had been relying on peanut butter. I'd used peanuts on Christopher Circle, but that had been more than fifteen years earlier. The fact that I'd forgotten only showed the extent of my obsession. I was distracted, harried, fuming. Then I remembered—peanuts!

So I set the squirrel trap behind the hedge out front, with a line of peanuts leading up to it and several more in a heap on the bait pan. And when I returned from campus for lunch one day, an angry Red Jimmy was rattling the bars of that cage. I'd finally caught one of the goddam sunnuvabitches!

What happened next was as comic as it was cruel. Determined to drown that sucker, I fetched a metal garbage can from the basement. There were two of them, both used to store kindling. But one of those had rusted out at the bottom from the flood and therefore leaked.

The other had lost one of its floppy metal handles, leaving a hole several inches from the top where the rivet had been. And this little rivet hole—like the hole in the proverbial Dutch dike—was suddenly preventing me from drowning my prisoner of war.

As I lowered the trap vertically into the garbage can and turned on the hose, the Red Jimmy scrambled to keep its head above water. But just when the water was about to cover the trap completely, it reached the level of that rivet hole and the garbage can began to pee, allowing the Red Jimmy to keep breathing.

Its dark eyes glared at me in a panic, mouth open, fangs bared, its toenails—with which it had scraped through our front step—grasping the wire bars of the trap so tightly I could feel the tension. I was trembling myself, because of another problem. In snapping shut, the trap had become a trapezoid. But when held in a vertical position, the end doors could flop open if not secured. And the squirrel could escape.

Struggling to keep its head above water, the Red Jimmy had wedged its nose against the trap's top door, which I was holding shut with both hands. The opposite end was held shut against the bottom of the garbage can. We'd reached a standoff—the hose was running, the garbage can was peeing, the Red Jimmy was still breathing, and I was maintaining my grip. And we could have gone on like that for hours.

There was only one thing to do—direct the flow of the hose right into the squirrel's mouth. Which I did with my right hand while holding the trap shut with my left—with every last ounce of my strength and anger—a pose I held for twenty minutes, a full ten minutes after that Red Jimmy began to turn slow sommersaults in its underwater casket.

Because it had drowned with its eyes open.

And was still glaring at me.

Ohio Ringside

A Requiem for Boxing in the Buckeye State

I am a licensed professional boxing judge in the state of Ohio. People who don't know boxing think I get in the ring with the boxers. No, I tell them. That's the referee. The three judges sit on stools just outside the ropes, each on a different side of the ring. The timekeeper, fight doctor, and supervisor from the Ohio Athletic Commission sit on the fourth side.

"But you're an English professor!" some people say, as if my vocation and avocation are mutually exclusive. Actually, I served an informal apprenticeship at Ohio Northern University by judging amateur bouts at Park Hall Fight Night—for seventeen years the number-one student charity fund-raiser—until the event was terminated on the advice of university attorneys.

I grew up in the 1950s watching boxing on television with my father and grandfather, live from Madison Square Garden in New York City. Watching boxing was in my blood. In 1962 we watched as Benet "Kid" Paret was beaten senseless by Emile Griffith, slipping into a coma after the fight and dying nine days later. In 1977 I was at the Capital Centre in Washington, D.C., to see Muhammad Ali fight Alfredo Angelista, a lackluster title bout that Ali won by unanimous decision in fifteen rounds, his best days already behind him.

I moved to Ohio in 1986, just after the glory years of Youngstown's Ray "Boom Boom" Mancini, whose fights I'd watched on national TV. Mancini rose to prominence in 1981 when he lost to lightweight champion Alexis Arguello in one of the most spectacular bouts of the decade. In May of 1982 he earned the title himself in a slugfest with Arturo Frias, retaining the crown in November of that same year when he battered the Korean fighter Duk Koo Kim into submission in the fourteenth round. Kim died from brain injuries five days later, and his mother committed suicide. As a result of the Kim fight, title bouts were reduced from fifteen rounds to twelve. After that fight, Mancini fell into a depression, never regaining his form. He later attempted a comeback, losing much-ballyhooed fights to Livingstone Bramble and Hector Camacho.

In 1988 I brought acclaimed author Joyce Carol Oates to Ohio Northern University for a reading. Oates had gained a measure of notoriety with her 1987 *Life* magazine interview with Mike Tyson. The media loved the unlikely duo—the fragile Princeton University intellectual and the hulking undefeated heavyweight. Building on that initial interview, later editions of Oates's 1987 book *On Boxing* devoted sixty-six pages to Tyson.

As I pointed out in my introduction of Oates to a packed house, she had been offered the job of boxing commissioner of New York— her home state—because of her lifelong interest in boxing. We talked boxing to and from the Columbus airport, and after her visit she sent me an autographed copy of *Reading the Fights: The Best Writing About the Most Controversial of Sports,* a 1988 collection of articles on the all-time classic bouts, a book she edited with Daniel Halpern.

But all media hype involving Oates and boxing abruptly evaporated when Tyson was convicted of rape and sentenced to three years in jail following his loss to Columbus native James "Buster" Douglas. Douglas, perhaps the only boxer most Ohioans are certain to know, was the journeyman fighter who stunned the boxing world in February of 1990 by knocking out Mike Tyson in Japan. Eight months later he lost his title to Evander Holyfield in a third-round knockout. Having earned twenty million dollars fighting Tyson, Douglas, a skilled fighter who lacked motivation and determination, was overweight and underprepared for the Holyfield fight. He later ballooned to 400 pounds before mustering a minor comeback.

During the early nineties, when I was judging amateur bouts at Ohio Northern, I met Rufus Brassell, a former heavyweight from nearby Lima, who often refereed at Park Hall Fight Night. Brassell had a record of 13–1 going into March 3, 1970, when he suffered a second-round knockout at the hands of Jerry Quarry—"the Great White Hope"—who later lost to both Joe Frazier and Muhammad Ali.

Back in the ring less than four weeks later, Brassell was pounded into a first-round technical knockout by George Foreman. Foreman went undefeated that year, winning eleven of his twelve bouts by knockout. He later lost the infamous "Rumble in the Jungle" to Ali, staged a series of comebacks, then retired for good—to hawk Meinecke Mufflers and the George Foreman Grill. Meanwhile, Rufus Brassell slipped into obscurity, retiring with a record of 18–7.

I first saw Aaron McLaurine, another Lima fighter, on television in the early nineties, when he was a last-minute opponent for a ranked middleweight. Born in 1971, McLaurine was in his prime but failed to take advantage of the national exposure. His nickname was "Showtime," but in that fight he was "Slowtime," unable—or unwilling—to let his hands fly. It was obvious that he didn't like to get hit, and he lost a unanimous decision in a decidedly dull bout that could have otherwise catapulted his career.

In 1997 I watched McLaurine fight in Findlay, knocking out his opponent in the seventh of eight rounds. He was a different fighter that night from the one I'd seen on television. There was a lot of hotdogging as he lived up to his nickname, but it was still obvious to me that he didn't like to get hit.

In 1998 I earned my judging license, and in 2003 I judged McLaurine's final fight—for the Great Lakes Boxing Federation super-middleweight title, one of many meaningless titles in a plethora of boxing jurisdictions. Fighting before a hometown crowd of about 600 in Lima's UAW hall, McLaurine was out of shape and showboated instead of boxed, but he still won a unanimous decision over a weak opponent.

McLaurine finished his career with a record of 23–19–5, the five draws dropping him a notch below a winning percentage. As with Buster Douglas, he was another Ohio might-have-been.

The latest Ohio hopeful is Devin Vargas of Toledo, an undefeated heavyweight as of this writing. Named the "Golden Boy" of the 2000 National Golden Gloves tournament after winning the heavyweight division, Vargas retained his Golden Gloves crown in 2001, then concluded a stellar amateur career by defeating Chazz Witherspoon to make the 2004 Olympic team, which he captained. But he lost a decision to Viktar Zuyev of Bellorussia in his second Olympic bout and finished out of the medals.

Vargas is 16–0 as a pro, with seven knockouts. His most recent victory was a first-round technical knockout of Philadelphia brawler Dave Brunelli in May of 2008, a fight broadcast on ESPN-2. According to Joe DeGuardia, head of Star Boxing, "Devin is a good young prospect and I expect big things out of him." But I'm not so sanguine about Vargas. Let me tell you why.

In October of 2005, Vargas, who was born in 1981, won a controversial majority decision in a four-round bout with Ed Perry in Chester, West Virginia. One reporter covering that fight described Vargas as "flabby looking"—exactly as he appeared twenty months later when I judged his six-round fight with Mijaheed Moore at the Riverfront Hotel in Toledo.

I was excited to learn that Vargas was on the card that night, because he'd been in the Ohio news so often during the 2004 Olympics. But I couldn't believe what I was seeing when he stepped into the ring. He was obviously out of shape, a soft belly bouncing at his belt, yet it didn't stop him from "showboating" to the hometown crowd. His antics could have cost him the fight—he was losing on points after the first two rounds—but he managed a few flashes of brilliance to earn a unanimous decision.

Like Buster Douglas before him, Vargas seems to lack motivation to train. His own recent history is against him, and he will have to dedicate himself more thoroughly as the quality of his opponents increases, if his Golden Boy career is to continue. After the fight in Toledo, Vargas won his next five fights before suffering his first loss in April 2009, a TKO at the hands of undefeated heavyweight Kevin Johnson. He returned to the ring in September of that year to win a unanimous decision over Terrell Nelson, a lackluster opponent with an 8–8 record.

On the distaff side, in stark contrast, is Vonda Ward, another Ohio heavyweight of the new millennium, who was born in Macedonia, southeast of Cleveland, in 1973. The former world heavyweight champion of the International Boxing Association, Ward was undefeated in twenty-one fights, with seventeen knockouts, before being knocked out in the first round by Ann Wolfe in Biloxi, Mississippi, on May 8, 2004, to lose her title in her only loss.

Ward played basketball at the University of Tennessee, then professionally in Europe and Colorado, before turning to boxing. On March 11, 2000, I judged her third professional bout, at the National Guard Armory in Findlay. It was a cold night, snowing heavily outside. Inside, old basketball hoops bracketed the ring in the smoky, dimly lit hall. Rock music bounced off the walls, and the lights kept going out because the sound system was too powerful for the antiquated electrical system.

Early in the evening, a few of the 500 fans who eventually showed up were milling about the empty rows of wooden folding chairs—drinking beer, eating sandwiches, and studying the mimeographed program—when Ward, who was scheduled for the fourth of seven bouts, slipped into the ring, already dressed to fight. Her short blonde hair flew as she bounced up and down to test the canvas and then fell back against the ropes to assess their give. She was the only fighter on the card to do so.

At a statuesque six-six and 190 pounds, decked out in star-spangled red, white, and blue, Ward—nicknamed "the All-American Girl"— was electrifying that night, dispensing with her opponent, Nicolyn Armstrong of Indianapolis, in fifty-eight seconds of the first round. Her height and long reach made it easy to establish her jab. Then she moved inside and dropped Armstrong with a series of devastating body shots—a quick, efficient, and totally impressive performance.

Intrigued by Ward's prospects, I followed her progress closely over the next few years, eventually interviewing her for an article for *Sports Illustrated for Women* when an editor expressed an interest in my query. Had I been called to judge any more of her bouts, I would have had to excuse myself due to a conflict of interest, but she began to fight more and more outside of Ohio—in Missouri, New York, Indiana, and elsewhere.

The last time I saw Ward fight in person was against GiGi Jackson, a four-time national amateur boxing champion, in February of 2002 at the Value City Arena on the Ohio State campus in Columbus, a bout televised by ESPN-2. The fans, nearly 8,000 strong, were divided in their allegiance, since Jackson had played basketball for the Buckeyes. Buster Douglas was in attendance, shaking hands and signing autographs. It was a grueling fight, won by Ward in a fourth-round technical knockout.

In what seemed a bad omen, *Sports Illustrated for Women* folded just as I was finishing my article on Vonda Ward. Then her undefeated string came to a heartbreaking end in Biloxi, when Ann Wolfe caught her flush on the chin in the opening round. Hitting the canvas hard, Ward was given oxygen, her neck was stabilized with a protective collar, and she was hospitalized. I watched the devastating knockout again and again in QuickTime on the Internet. In the aftermath of the fight, there were calls for Ward to retire, but she returned to the ring eight months later to knock out veteran fighter Marsha Valley in Cleveland.

Unlike Douglas, McLaurine, and Vargas, Ward's devotion to boxing is total. As Pat Summitt, the legendary Tennessee basketball coach informed me by e-mail, "I am proud of Vonda Ward, and I am certainly not surprised at her dedication and commitment to her boxing career. When she makes up her mind to do something, she has the incredible focus and drive that it takes to make it happen."

Ward told me she hopes to get into sports modeling when she retires. She'd be a natural—her blonde hair is now long, her body is still perfectly toned, and her face is reminiscent of the young Jane Fonda. Has the time come for her to step down from the ring? We can only wait and see. Following her win over Marsha Valley, Ward added four more victories through 2008, dropping out of the heavyweight division to win, and successfully defend, the IBA cruiserweight title.

Meanwhile, it's apparent that professional boxing is deteriorating in Ohio, if measured by the number of amateur Toughman Contests held these days as opposed to the number of pro cards. Mixed Martial Arts—a combination of boxing, kick-boxing, and wrestling—has become increasingly popular as well, given its prime-time exposure on national television. Although I have no interest in judging MMA, I've judged more than my share of Toughman tussles at a variety of venues around the Ohio Outback—from the Allen County Fairgrounds and Marion Coliseum to Dayton and Toledo.

A national program of competition, the Toughman Contests—sometimes billed as Tough*person* due to the number of women who want to mix it up in the ring—are the best-attended boxing events in the nation. According to *Toughman Contest History*, boxing fans get to see what they want: "the hometown boys, the real amateurs. The seasoned street fighters with little or no boxing skill but lots of guts . . . punching it out in the ring, in front of their friends and family, for a little fame and fortune."

The first Toughman World Championship, held in Detroit's Silverdome, drew 30,000 fans from across the nation, with a $50,000 first prize. At the local level, the winner of a given weight class might walk away with $600. Unsung professionals don't pocket much more.

In Ohio, Toughman bouts are held on two consecutive nights because of a state rule that prevents fighters from boxing more than nine rounds in twenty-four hours. Each bout consists of three one-minute rounds, whereas professional male boxers fight three-minute rounds and professional women fight two-minute rounds.

While judging professional bouts is difficult enough—especially when fighters are evenly matched—judging Toughman bouts can be next to impossible. Scoring for both is on the Ten-Point Must System. The winner of a round is awarded ten points, the loser nine or less. A knockdown is scored as a ten-eight round. Two knockdowns make it ten-seven. Even rounds (ten-ten) are discouraged.

But many Toughman fights are total mismatches, with someone getting knocked silly in a matter of seconds, rendering the judges' decision moot. Too often, however, especially when fighters are inept or out of shape, decisions are virtually arbitrary due to flailing arms, clinching, and no semblance of offense or defense whatsoever. Contestants charge like bulls, turn their backs on one another when hit, lose their protective headgear or mouthpieces or both. One night I saw a fighter lose his padded groin protector.

In January of 2005, on the second evening of a Toughman event I'd been assigned to judge at the Hara Arena in Dayton, a twenty-seven-year-old heavyweight, and father of several children, was hospitalized following his bout and died during the night. I had judged his

Friday-night elimination bouts but was not on hand for Saturday's tragic fight. Having witnessed on television the devastation that led to the deaths of Paret and Kim, I don't know how I would have reacted had I seen that fighter carried from the ring.

Statistically, however, far more athletes die playing football each year than ever die in the ring. Toughman Contests have stricter safety precautions than professional boxing. All fighters must pay a fee to enter. They must pass a physical, wear protective gear, and use sixteen-ounce gloves, twice the weight worn by professional boxers.

But professional boxing, the sport that journalist A. J. Liebling dubbed "the sweet science," is just that—a subtle dance of self defense, an ebb and flow of courage and counterpunch, a test of wills and endurance. I keep on judging in hopes of finding the next great Ohio fighter.

And I think I may have found him. At a Toughman Contest, no less.

During the course of two evenings in early February of 2008, at a Toughman event in Toledo, I watched from my stool at ringside as a muscular and chiseled Tim Washington—six-six and 260 pounds—demolished all three of his opponents in a matter of seconds. In each bout he threw no more than three or four machinelike punches.

Inside the ropes the twenty-seven-year-old from Toledo is all stone-faced business, greeting his opponent with a baleful stare reminiscent of Sonny Liston. Outside the ring he flashes a smile like Tiger Woods. I later learned that Washington had lost a close decision to Justin Jones of Houston, Texas, in a bruising elimination bout during the 2007 Olympic trials in Salt Lake City. A victory would have put him on the U.S. boxing team as a super-heavyweight for the 2008 Olympics in Beijing.

After the Toughman fights concluded in Toledo, I followed Washington into the locker room to ask why he wasn't boxing professionally.

"I don't know how to go about finding a manager," he told me.

Before he left the arena, I got his phone number and went straight to Jamie Howe, one of two referees working the event that evening. Howe, who manages the boxing career of his brother, said he'd be happy to take Washington on. The next morning I phoned Washington to tell him the good news, but as of this writing I haven't been back in touch.

I'm just not ready for another Ohio boxing heartbreak.

Yard Wars of the Ohio Outback

Capitulation

The squirrel wars ended in a draw—a prolonged cease-fire—negotiated with the help of a sixteen-ounce plastic squirt bottle of Squirrel Scoot, a product I discovered when the New Leaf Nursery opened just north of town.

Stopping in after Thanksgiving to check out Christmas trees, I recognized a bottle of Ro-don't (or was it Ro-pel?), which I'd used years earlier to keep the neighbors' cats from shitting in the driveway. The label, as I've said, contained small Disneylike pictures of what the product repelled—armadillos, badgers, birds, cats, chipmunks, deer, gophers, moles, mice, prairie dogs, rabbits, raccoons, rats—everything but squirrels. But beside it on the shelf was a new product with *squirrel* in the brand name!

The Squirrel Scoot label sported a colorful cartoonish drawing of a bluebird happily singing in a birdfeeder—its song represented by a pair of sixteenth notes—as an unhappy squirrel scooted away, mouth open, its startled eyes watering. Squirrel Scoot had 99.892 percent inert ingredients, but its active ingredient—a mere 0.108 percent of the stuff—was capsaicin, an insidious compound produced as a metabolite of chili peppers. Capsaicin makes red pepper hotter than hot. It's what makes you holler after eating jalapeños. Applied monthly to the base of every tree in the yard, Squirrel Scoot lived up to its name.

But other yard wars continued in the years to follow, slowly breaking my spirit.

Like the label on the Squirrel Scoot container, our yard had hosted happy bluebirds for years—until one spring a pair of feisty sparrows claimed the birdhouse. And the bluebirds, not known for aggressiveness, nested elsewhere. As if to celebrate, the sparrows pecked open a side door in the birdhouse! I couldn't believe it. The hole I'd so lovingly cut into the plywood face of the bluebird house wasn't good enough for them. They wanted a second entrance. And so they built one.

Not long after I discovered that second hole, I saw four sparrows flitting about the birdhouse, coming and going, taking turns standing on the roof, ducking in and out. They'd turned the place into a condo! Angered over the loss of my bluebirds, I stuffed a cork from a wine bottle into that side entrance. But the sparrows uncorked it.

"Leave 'em alone," Elaine said. "At least we have birds."

"*All Creatures Great and Small*," I said cynically, quoting the title of an old sentimental bestseller.

Still, each winter I opened the face of that birdhouse and cleaned out its nests, tossing them into the corn stubble, hoping for a fresh start with bluebirds in the spring. And one year—ever so briefly—I noticed a pair of bluebirds atop the birdhouse. But a pair of sparrows arrived like dive-bombers and drove them off. Later that day, when I angrily opened the front of the birdhouse to discard what I assumed would be a fresh sparrow's nest, a female bluebird flew out in my face. Bluebirds had reclaimed the birdhouse after all! Only to abandon it after my rude intervention.

They never returned. And sparrows rule that birdhouse to this day.

. . .

If the sparrows broke my spirit, the swimming pool broke my back.

The pool and all of the equipment in the pool shed went to the university colleague whose car had slid into the Allens' ditch during the ice storm. He came one summer with his son to dismantle it, after I'd advertised the 24,000-gallon pool as "free for the taking."

But trying to eliminate the circle of dirt left behind by that pool dismantled *me*, exacerbating a back injury I'd first sustained when lifting a balled Christmas tree from the trunk of the Nova. Which I then aggravated when lifting a rolled-up carpet I'd brought home on the roof of the Caprice to unroll in the Florida room. The university's Maintenance Department had been recarpeting the hallways in my office building, and the industrial-grade stuff was "free for the taking."

Which gave me the idea to advertise the pool in the same way. Proving that there is, so to speak, no such thing as a free lunch. Not when it results in medical bills.

The coup de grâce—or coup de back, to be exact—occurred when I borrowed Chip's rototiller to rototill the ring of dirt beneath the pool liner once the pool was gone. The goal was to plant Kentucky Bluegrass. But Chip's gas-powered rototiller shook me to the bone as it rattled me back and forth across that circuslike ring—reducing me to a clown in the process—squeezing the already-bulging cartilage between my fourth and fifth lumbar vertebrae into a classic herniated disk.

It took me six months to recover from my laminectomy—the fancy name for "back surgery"—during which I had to hire Neal to mow our acre. Neal and Amy were both teachers, and therefore free in the summer, which is when Neal ran his landscaping business. He'd invested in one of those monster riding mowers that you see on golf courses. It would knock off our entire acre in twenty minutes, except for the ditches, of course, for which I offered the Lawn Boy.

The only thing more painful than a herniated disk is watching someone else mow your own lawn. And paying forty bucks a pop for the privilege.

. . .

During my months of convalescence, poison ivy took root beneath the long hedge out front, creeping through it like a thief and gradually working its way to the surface, leaving me scratching my arms and itching like mad—once I was able to work in the yard again—whenever I trimmed the hedge. Until I discovered the shiny-leafed interloper.

As with the squirrels, the poison ivy could only be contained, not eliminated, although I sprayed it with every New Leaf product that claimed it would kill it. Then I bought a pair of leather gloves and tried to yank the stuff out by the roots, burning the gloves afterward. But the creepy vines returned. All I could do was watch for them each year and snip them off at ground level before they could entwine themselves around the interior branches of the hedge.

I'd always felt victorious if all such battles could be confined to the yard. But then, for several years in a row, they moved *inside*— into the Florida room at first, then throughout the house—due to a statewide infestation of Asian lady beetles, which made the invasion of the seventeen-year locusts on Christopher Circle seem like a tea party. These orange-colored critters were twice the size of the harmless little red ladybugs I'd known as a kid. They bore a black dot on each wing, a bit like a fire ant, and smelled like a cigarette butt when crushed between thumb and finger.

Introduced into the United States via some sort of pest control project, Asian lady beetles swarmed across Ohio by the thousands, seeking interior corners in winter and crawling up the sliding glass doors of the Florida room the rest of the year. You could kill them with a fly swatter, but then you had to vacuum them up. So we kept a plugged-in hand-vac out in the Florida room, sucking up the suckers directly, several times daily, then spraying the air for the stench they left behind after being sucked up en masse.

In winter we plugged the hand-vac into an outlet in the family room, where we'd have to interrupt a video or television program to suck the suckers off the screen. Or off the long narrow windows at the east end of the room, where they'd alight as the morning sun warmed them. These orange-shelled black-dotted creatures slipped into every crevice, nook, and cranny—I found them in my underwear drawer, on my toothbrush, in my shoes—so often that it was useless to curse them.

Goddam . . . ! Whatever.

The only consolation was that everyone else had them, too.

"They're coming out of the woodwork!" Adrian said, calling home from college. Like Owen before him, Adrian had attended the university in town for two years, then transferred. Owen had graduated from Ohio State and was now based in Milwaukee, working for the U.S. Forest Service. Adrian was in his senior year at Ohio University in Athens. And their leaving home had automatically ended another yard war that had bugged me throughout their high school years— TP'ing. A local rite of passage with which I'd soon lost patience.

. . . sunnuvabitch kids!

The toilet paper attacks had always occurred in the dead of night after the Friday high school football games, costing me hours on Saturday morning—on my extension ladder in our forty trees pulling down the white streamers twisting in the wind, unable to reach half of them, of course, while Owen and Adrian slept in, having been out late themselves at the game and postgame parties. I was too impatient to roust them. If I did, they were too tired and grumpy to be of much help.

The first few times our yard got TP'd, I thought *OK, ha, ha. You got us!* But when it continued week after week—sometimes Owen was the intended "victim," sometimes Adrian—I began to feel, as with the squirrels, a bit paranoid. Fortunately, the toilet-papering stopped as soon as the boys moved out.

. . .

Late one summer, after several weeks of drought—when a wall of corn stood high across the backyard—I slipped outside to burn a pile of brush and sticks that had accumulated in the burning pen. The wind was unusually quiet, and I thought I'd take advantage of the opportunity. But the wind soon picked up.

Having balled up some newspapers and started the fire, I'd ducked in for lunch. Then I went out to the mailbox. Later, when I happened to peer into the backyard through the Florida room, I was entranced by what I saw. Rippling shapes were dancing in the shadows of the trees, from the apple trees to the badminton court. The leaping figures were mesmerizing. Until I realized they were flames. Orange, red, and yellow flames!

There was no smoke—the grass and leaves and corn were all too dry for that—just leaping flames, scorching a black swath from where the pool had once been over to the bluebird house, while making popcorn of the first few rows of corn in the field behind the burning pen. Fortunately, the hose was handy and I was able to contain the blaze, stamping out the low-running flames in the grass, trampling the corn, and spraying the leaves in the trees.

"Dad," Owen said, calling from Milwaukee, "you made two classic errors. First, you started a fire in dry conditions. Second, you left it unattended. Where was Mom?"

"At work," I said lamely.

As part of his job at the Forest Service, Owen had been trained to fight fires, occasionally getting called up for the big blazes out West. In quieter times he dressed up as Smokey the Bear for a variety of educational events.

One summer—the one I always remind him of when he reminds *me* of burning down the backyard—he went dressed as Smokey the Bear to a professional baseball game at Milwaukee County Stadium. During the seventh-inning stretch, he was to race around the bases with a guy dressed as a hot dog and another dressed as a bratwurst. Smokey's costume was so complicated that Owen had an assistant to help him dress. But the assistant was dawdling and the seventh-inning stretch was dwindling when Owen finally headed for first base, losing his suspenders en route. Dropping Smokey's blue dungarees to his ankles.

Owen never lived it down at the office. Smokey the Bear is a serious symbol not to be taken lightly.

"Good thing your head was covered," I laughed.

"Good thing *you* had your hose handy," he retorted.

. . .

After years of battling the forces of nature in the yard and within the house itself, I never thought I'd have to fight a war *on top of* the house. But I did.

One evening during our eighteenth summer on County Road 50, when Elaine and I were in the empty nest stage of our life, with retirement on the horizon, I happened to glance up at the roof out front to find it streaked with ugly brown stains. They had appeared quite suddenly. Whatever the cause, I didn't appreciate it. We were preparing to put the house up for sale in order to downsize.

"Those dingy stains are caused by algae," the head of the Biology Department told me. "It won't harm anything, but the moss that feeds on it will. It attaches itself to the granules in the shingles, which come off when you kill it, shortening the life of your roof."

"Kill it?" I said. "How?"

"With any good oxygenated cleaner."

There was only one thing to do—go to Furrows, where the clerk, of course, had just what I needed for attacking that moss. Oxi-Clean Versatile Stain Remover.

Bolted to the exterior wall of Owen's bedroom was a narrow ladderlike tower that held our TV antenna and gave access to the roof. Putting on the kneepads I used when cleaning leaves from the gutters, or creeping around in the crawl space, I climbed up and scrubbed the shingles like a charwoman, repeatedly dipping a scrub brush into a bucket of water spiked with Oxi-Clean Versatile Stain Remover, which, according to the label, was "a safe alternative to chlorine bleach." Dragging the hose up the tower ladder behind me, I rinsed the suds into the gutters as I worked my way across the roof at the front of the house.

But the battle was harder than expected. The rust-colored stains—caused by brown moss clinging to the shingles—had spread down the roof whenever it rained. A single scrubbing wasn't enough to remove them. I had to repeat the process—twice a day, three days in a row, in the heat of the summer sun—scraping the deposits of moss from each shingle with a putty knife, then scrubbing away with the Oxi-Clean Versatile Stain Remover. After which the roof looked like its old self, minus a few million shingle granules that had rolled into the gutters. And my back felt like I'd popped another disk.

"I'm getting too old for this," I told Elaine.

So when clover appeared in the yard, I began to capitulate.

Like the moss, the clover came suddenly. It was simply there one spring, a small patch by the hedge out front. But it had already begun to spread around the side of the house to the badminton court by the time I noticed it. For a brief moment I felt lucky, getting down on my hands and knees to look for a four-leaf clover. I didn't find one, of course, which made me feel unlucky. Because that clover began to insinuate itself everywhere. Year after year. I got so I could recognize the new recruits in the spring—lacy yellow buds that popped up here and there, then matured into tough green cloverleaves, working their way through the blades of grass like the poison ivy in the hedge.

I never realized how clover grows until I took a screwdriver to it, slipping it just beneath the surface of the grass. Lifting carefully, I discovered a network of thread-like vines, anchored at intervals by thin roots six inches deep. After a rain I could pull those roots easily, loosening the soil with my screwdriver then ripping out the threadlike network. But I couldn't keep up with it. Unlike the algae-eating moss, I couldn't kill it.

Nor, like the squirrels and poison ivy, could I contain it. Despite blasting it with every alleged clover-killing product on the market.

The capitulation came when I called ChemLawn, the lawn service I'd abandoned on Christopher Circle. In the interim, the cost of a single application had tripled. But we had to sign up. I'd worn smooth the blade of several screwdrivers fighting clover year after year. And I was growing weary of the hand-to-hand combat. I needed reinforcements, and ChemLawn was worth the money. It blasted that clover from our acre in a single season.

. . .

But the greatest capitulation—a psychological blow—came when Furrows, my faithful ally in Lima, was bought out, demolished, and replaced by a gigantic Home Depot. I suppose I should have felt happy, because Home Depot doubled the square footage of the old building, thereby doubling the arsenal for my yard wars. But after two decades as a homeowner in the Ohio Outback, I was suffering from battle fatigue. And rather than exhilaration when I heard the news, I felt depressed.

"What's wrong?" Elaine said.

"You can't win," I replied. "When it comes to yard wars, all you can do is put up a good fight. But you can't win."

It took a tornado to drive that lesson home.

It came late one Sunday afternoon while I was taking a dozen students in a university van back to campus from a literary field trip. We'd been studying Thurber, who'd written about his family's antics at their Columbus home. So a field trip to the Thurber House was the perfect extracurricular activity.

But on the return trip one of the students happened to check with her roommate by cell phone to learn some startling news—a concert in progress at the university's Performing Arts Center had just been interrupted. A tornado had been spotted in the vicinity. Everyone was seeking shelter underground. Meanwhile, we were three miles from campus, in open farmland of the Great Black Swamp, on a long straight stretch of road flanked by deep ditches. The wind was fierce, and the sky around us had turned from black to yellow.

"Watch for the funnel!" I told the students. "If you see it, give a yell! I'll stop the van and we'll dive in the ditch!"

Fortunately, our university town sits in a shallow depression, which encourages tornados to skip over the area. Such was the case with this one. But the winds at its periphery snapped yet another large branch from the big swamp maple at the front of our badminton court. Slamming it into the roof of the Florida room. It also ripped up a line of trees through the local cemetery. "I'm getting too old for this," I told Elaine the following morning, climbing the TV antenna tower to the roof with my electric chain saw. "I'm gonna put in for early retirement."

So we began scouting condos and retirement communities. Then I went to Home Depot and bought a large sign—FOR SALE BY OWNER. But one night, as we prepared to put the house on the market, I woke in a sweat and nudged Elaine.

"Whatzamadder?" she muttered.

"I don't want to move," I said. "I'll miss the yard."

Elaine rolled over and sat up. "But the yard drives you *mad*."

"I know," I said. "But it's—*therapy*."

"Go to sleep," she said. "We'll discuss it in the morning."